Purdue University Monographs in Romance Languages

Volume 23

PETER V. CONROY Jr.

INTIMATE, INTRUSIVE AND TRIUMPHANT
Readers in the *Liaisons Dangereuses*

JOHN BENJAMINS PUBLISHING COMPANY

INTIMATE, INTRUSIVE, AND TRIUMPHANT

PURDUE UNIVERSITY MONOGRAPHS IN ROMANCE LANGUAGES

William M. Whitby, General Editor
Allan H. Pasco, Editor for French
Enrique Caracciolo-Trejo, Editor for Spanish

Associate Editors

I. French

Max Aprile, Purdue University
Paul Benhamou, Purdue University
Willard Bohn, Illinois State University
Gerard J. Brault, Pennsylvania State University
Germaine Brée, Wake Forest University
Jules Brody, Harvard University
Victor Brombert, Princeton University
Ursula Franklin, Grand Valley State College
Floyd F. Gray, University of Michigan
Gerald Herman, University of California, Davis
Michael Issacharoff, University of Western Ontario
Thomas E. Kelly, Purdue University
Milorad R. Margitić, Wake Forest University
Bruce A. Morrissette, University of Chicago
Roy Jay Nelson, University of Michigan
Glyn P. Norton, Pennsylvania State University
David Lee Rubin, University of Virginia
Murray Sachs, Brandeis University
English Showalter, Rutgers University, Camden
Donald Stone, Jr., Harvard University

II. Spanish

J.B. Avalle-Arce, University of California, Santa Barbara
Rica Brown, M.A., Oxon
Frank P. Casa, University of Michigan
James O. Crosby, Florida International University
Alan D. Deyermond, Westfield College (University of London)
David T. Gies, University of Virginia
Roberto González Echevarría, Yale University
Thomas R. Hart, University of Oregon
David K. Herzberger, University of Connecticut
Djelal Kadir II, Purdue University
John W. Kronik, Cornell University
Floyd F. Merrell, Purdue University
Geoffrey Ribbans, Brown University
Elias L. Rivers, SUNY, Stony Brook
Francisco Ruiz Ramón, University of Chicago
J.M. Sobré, Indiana University
Bruce W. Wardropper, Duke University

Volume 23

Peter V. Conroy Jr.

Intimate, Intrusive and Triumphant
Readers in the 'Liaisons Dangereuses'

PETER V. CONROY, JR.

INTIMATE, INTRUSIVE, AND TRIUMPHANT

Readers in the *Liaisons dangereuses*

JOHN BENJAMINS PUBLISHING COMPANY
Amsterdam/Philadelphia

1987

Library of Congress Cataloging in Publication Data

Conroy, Peter V.
  Intimate, intrusive, and triumphant.

  (Purdue University monographs in Romance languages, ISSN 0165-8743; v. 23)
1. Laclos, Choderlos de, 1741-1803. Liaisons dangereuses. 2. Laclos, Choderlos de, 1741-1803 -- Technique. 3. Authors and readers. I. Title. II. Series.
PQ1993.L22L5467   1987   843'.6   87-9185
ISBN 90 272 1733 5 (European) / ISBN 0-915027-72-0 (US) (alk. paper)

© Copyright 1987 - John Benjamins B.V.
No part of this book may be reproduced in any form, by print, photoprint, microfilm, or any other means, without written permission from the publisher.

Contents

Preface: Pentecost: The Feast of the Reader .... *vii*

    Scope and Aims .... *ix*

1. Introduction to the Fictional Reader 1

       Definition of the Fictional Reader 1
       Editeur, Rédacteur, and Mme de Rosemonde 3
       The Postal System: Privileging the Addressee 7
       Reading: The Power of the Word 9

2. A Theory of Fictional Readers and Their Reading 11

       Awareness of the Reader 11
       The Bonds of Confidence 15
       Receiving and Responding 26
       The Dangers of Reading 35
       Writing/Reading: The Ultimate Act 39

3. Hidden Readers 49

       Valmont: The Reader as Thief 53
       The Invited Intruder: Mme de Merteuil 64

4. Split Personalities: Characterizing Writers and Readers 81

       Cécile Volanges 81
       Mme de Volanges 84
       The Chevalier Danceny 88
       Mme de Rosemonde 93

Intimate, Intrusive, and Triumphant

5. Writer vs. Reader: The Struggle for Power 97

    The Written Battle Lines. 98
    The Readerly Armageddon 105
    The Moral Reader 119

Notes 125

Selected Bibliography. 131
    The Text 131
    Secondary Readings. 131

Preface

Pentecost: The Feast of the Reader

The miracle of Pentecost is not just a theological phenomenon; it is also a literary event of the highest magnitude which can serve as introduction as well as illustration for the present study, which is concerned with the question of the fictional reader imbedded inside the text he is reading. The description of Pentecost in the Acts of the Apostles reads as follows:

> And when the day of Pentecost was fully come, they were all with one accord in one place. And suddenly there came a sound from heaven as of a rushing mighty wind, and it filled all the house where they were sitting. And there appeared unto them cloven tongues like as of fire, and it sat upon each of them. And they were all filled with the Holy Ghost, and began to speak with other tongues, as the Spirit gave them utterance. And there were dwelling at Jerusalem Jews, devout men, out of every nation under heaven. Now when this was noised abroad, the multitude came together, and were confounded, because that every man heard them speak in his own language. And they were all amazed and marvelled, saying one to another, Behold, are not all these which speak Galilaeans? And how hear we every man in our own tongue, wherein we were born? Parthians, and Medes, and Elamites, and the dwellers in Mesopotamia, and in Judaea, and Cappadocia, in Pontus, and Asia, Phrygia, and Pamphylia, in Egypt, and in the parts of Libya around Cyrene, and strangers of Rome, Jews and proselytes, Cretes and Arabians, we do hear them speak in our tongues the wonderful works of God. And they were all amazed.[1]

The theological question posed in this passage involves the nature of the Spirit's gift. When the Apostles speak, do they in fact speak in different languages, in tongues they themselves do not know? The long-standing tradition which pictures (literally, since painters have rendered the scene visually in these same terms) the Pentecostal event as the descent of the Holy Spirit in the form of tongues of fire upon the heads of the Apostles would support the interpretation that they did indeed speak in different languages simultaneously.

The phrase "speaking in tongues" means precisely that: one is able to speak a new and even heretofore unknown language. The other possibility, and the one that interests us in our present context, is that the Apostles' audience *heard* them in various languages while the Apostles themselves spoke their own dialect. The text says: "every man heard them speak in his own language." A more modern translation renders it: "they heard them each in his own language."[2] According to this second possibility, the miracle of Pentecost would take place within the listeners. The Apostles speak their own Galilean dialect while each listener hears them in his own native language.

The literary question concealed in this theological dilemma (which in fact does not present any problem for theologians, but simply offers them room for speculation) is basic to the present study. Translated from theological to literary terms, the miracle of Pentecost is the reception of the text. Pentecost is the perfect communication, an exemplary message perceived and understood as fully and as completely as originally intended. It is transparency itself, a message which loses nothing in transmission, a message which is totally efficacious. Nothing impedes this crystaline process, this movement of the message, of the Word—appropriately, literary and theological vocabulary reinforce each other here: the Word is the Good News which is the Gospel itself and, according to John, the Word is God Himself—from the speaking Apostles to their listening masses, eager for conversion and ready to accept their words and the Word. For the literary critic, then, the question here is one of narrative emphasis. Is Pentecost a narrator's feast, the celebration of the Apostles who miraculously acquire the ability to speak in a manner heretofore unknown to them? Or is it an example of the reader and the listener at work, receiver and receptor, those Parthians, Medes, Elamites, and dwellers in Mesopotamia who give life to the word by hearing and accepting it?

> And they were all amazed, and were in doubt, saying one to another, What meaneth this?[3]

Traditionally, Pentecost commemorates the public mission, the missionary stage of the early Church. From this day forth, the Apostles will go out and preach and bring the Good News, the Gospel, the Word, to those who have not yet heard it. Pentecost is therefore a sublimely literary celebration, too. The Word is a text, the Good News a discourse, and in this primary and defining action of their ministry, the Apostles present a paradigm of the narrative act which transfers a message from speaker to listener, from writer to reader. The description of Pentecost we have cited comes from the Acts of the Apostles, also known as the Book of Acts. In our literary context, these titles are richly significant. Words and deeds are joined and equalized: discourse is action, and action discourse.

Here we will not even dare attempt to resolve the exact theological meaning of "speaking in tongues." Rather, we choose simply to point out the tremendous importance of Pentecost as a literary event and especially as an example of reader reception in practice. Pentecost is the initial feast, the commemoration of the beginning of a religion based on the "Good Book," the ultimate text, whose subject, God Almighty, is defined at the opening of John's Gospel in grammatical terms, as the Word. For us, the significance of Pentecost lies partially in its critical affirmation of the twin poles of the narrative process, of their symmetrical and complementary nature, and of the difficulty in distinguishing between them. In addition to its most important religious connotations, then, Pentecost speaks directly to the literary process, to contemporary literary theory, and to the topic of the present study, the presence of the fictional reader inside the text that creates him and the role of his reading activity in the overall narrative strategy.

Scope and Aims

It might seem incongruous to some readers that after having pitched this theoretical invocation of the receiving function, of the reader's role, on the high ground of Sacred Scripture, we should now announce that the novel in which we will examine this technical phenomenon is Choderlos de Laclos's libertine masterpiece, *Les Liaisons dangereuses*. Such a juxtaposition contains nothing shocking, however. For those acquainted with the French licentious novel of the eighteenth century, the mingling of the sacred and the profane is rather commonplace. Valmont often has recourse to such a mixture of tones and inspirations when he describes Mme de Tourvel, the object of his lust, as "divine" or as an "angel."

Published early in 1782, this novel summed up and perfected the entire tradition of the *roman libertin* that had flourished throughout the eighteenth century. Part of this role as summation is due to historical accident: the *Liaisons* precedes the French Revolution by only a few years and is therefore one of the last novels of its genre to be written before that social, political, and moral upheaval. When calm returned to France after the Napoleonic adventure, the society that nourished the characters and the life-style we find in the *Liaisons* had disappeared, while the mood and perspective of *auteurs libertins* like Laclos were replaced by Romantic feeling and *sensibilité*. Paradoxically, this novel was also, in the words of Martin Turnell, the "betrayal" of that same libertine life-style which it exemplified so brilliantly.[4] Even before Turnell, critics had debated the moral message of the *Liaisons*. On one side were those who saw in the novel a critical and moral judgment about the corrupt society it described, while on the other stood those who claimed that the novel was, because of its powerful evocation of vice, a source of danger itself and therefore a corrupting force in its own right. Despite the passion and persuasion of the partisans of both viewpoints, the question still remains an open one today.

Choderlos de Laclos was a military man, an artillery general who fought in the Republican Army and later served under Napoleon in Italy where he died in 1803. He was also the personal secretary to the Duc d'Orléans, Philippe Egalité, in the early days of the Revolution. The *Liaisons* is his only novel although he did write some poetry, a treatise on the education of women, and various political pamphlets for Orléans. Consequently, there is a profound mystery surrounding this novel without origin or sequel, this nearly perfect literary masterpiece by an amateur who never produced another work which could even hint at the power and the mastery of this single shot. Nothing in Laclos's biography prepares us for the *Liaisons,* nor can we find in his other papers and correspondences any real clues to his masterpiece or reflections on its genesis.

Ever since its publication in 1782, readers have been seeking in the *Liaisons* the real individuals, the historical personages whom Laclos was supposed to have copied and reproduced in his only slightly fictionalized version of life in a French garrison town. Grenoble, of course, has been identified as that town, and various names have been proposed as models for Mme de Merteuil, the Vicomte de Valmont, Cécile Volanges, and others.[5]

These are but a few of the numerous avenues that a study of Laclos and his *Liaisons dangereuses* could take. The recent outpouring of critical interest in this novel further attests to the topic's richness and variety. In this study, however, I will concentrate on the one aspect of this multi-faceted novel that I have already evoked as the literary counterpart of the Pentecostal experience: the question of the fictional reader.[6] Consequently I will not be concerned with Laclos's biography, nor with the identification of the real figures behind the *clés* and their fictional veneer, nor even with the position of the *Liaisons* in the development of the epistolary genre or in the libertine tradition. My focus is consciously narrow.[7] I propose to study only how this text functions when it is consistently analyzed from that single viewpoint of the fictional reader inside the text. My purpose in adopting so rigid and so concentrated a perspective is twofold. First, I intend to demonstrate conclusively that although the fictional reader has gone largely unnoticed, he or she has in fact a critical function and a major role in the intense struggle of wills that Laclos depicts in his novel. Indeed, I will eventually go so far as to claim that the reader, by the very fact of his or her reading, becomes the most powerful character in the *Liaisons,* more powerful than the narrator, who is usually considered the motor and the vital force in any novel. Secondly, I hope to reconcile the unfortunate dichotomy that has split recent literary studies and set partisans of the *nouvelle critique* against "traditionalists" by showing how the concerns of one group can in fact coincide with, and complement, the interests of the other. My discussion of form and technique as seen from the perspective of the reader will produce results that are compatible with traditional interpretations; on occasion, I hope to arrive at some "new" insights, made possible by this perspective, which will resolve or at least speak pertinently to issues that traditional criticism is still debating. One very simple example I can offer immediately is the question of Valmont's duel with Danceny and the logical incorporation of that incident into the novel's story line. Seen as a consequence of readers and their reading, this duel acquires a substance and a necessary relation to other incidents in the plot (i.e., Merteuil's disfigurement) that are impossible to minimize but which are evident only from such a perspective.

To focus exclusively and steadily on the fictional reader in a novel is an enormously difficult task, because this reader is but an implied presence, a shadowy, almost invisible figure whom we shall have to ferret out of his hiding places. Hence all that we say about him or her will be the product of induction and inference. Furthermore, in an epistolary novel like the *Liaisons*, reading is the basic enabling activity of the genre: without the justification provided by reading, the logic of the novel would dissolve and the fiction disintegrate. Thus the particular and subtle distinctions among the various fictional readers risk being eclipsed by the overall thrust that the very fact of reading imparts to the entire novel. Nonetheless, despite these dangers, the temptation to try to seize this long-unrecognized and decidedly slippery reader is a powerful one. In making that attempt, it is hoped that something both different and valuable will be added to the canon of Laclos studies.

The ultimate purpose of the present study, then, is to bring some contemporary methodological tools to the traditional task of making sense of the complex and variegated text that is the *Liaisons dangereuses*. Without apologizing for or diminishing my intention to provide a distinctly contemporary reading, I also want to insist on my conviction that even such "new" methods will eventually harmonize with the long-standing interpretations of this novel. My interest in the fictional reader will, I am convinced, lead to new explanations for the behavior and the characterizations that critics have always observed. In short, I hope to keep the best of traditional interpretations and add to them the additional insights that the fictional reader will provide.

1

Introduction to the Fictional Reader

Definition of the Fictional Reader

By its very nature as a fiction composed of a series of letters, written most often by several different characters who send them to each other, the epistolary novel privileges the symmetrical and complementary roles of narrator and narratee, of writer and reader, more than any other novelistic format. The concept of "narrator" is well known, since interest in narrative point of view has been very strong in critical circles for at least the past fifty years. The idea of the "narratee" is much less familiar. The French term *narrataire* dates back to an article by Gerald Prince.[1] Its English translation "narratee" is more or less synonymous with other words that have imposed themselves on the critical vocabulary: *destinataire*, addressee, implied reader, fictional reader, intended reader.[2] The concept of a receptor who is symmetrically opposed to an emitter springs from Roman Jakobson's classic essay, "Linguistique et poétique,"[3] in which he identifies, among the elements constituting a valid communication, an *addresser* who sends or encodes the message and an *addressee* who receives or decodes it. When applied to the novel, Jakobson's model produces a narrator who tells or recounts the story and a narratee who listens to that telling. Continuing this emphasis on the reader/receptor, contemporary linguists like Emile Benveniste have shown that the speaking subject, the individual who uses the first person singular pronoun "I," implicitly recognizes an indirect object, another individual spoken to, a second person "you" to whom he is addressing his comments.[4] More recent literary critics like Susan Lanser[5] and Seymour Chatman[6] have discussed in greater detail the functioning of the narratee and the advantages of using the concept as a critical tool in analyzing novels.

As welcome as this new attention to the presence of the addressee may be, it has not as yet focused on the most rewarding instances of the fictional reader at work. While the addressee remains a useful theoretical concept in dealing with traditional novelistic formats like nineteenth-century third person omniscient narrations, it becomes an imperative consideration in an epistolary novel. The difficulties and the rewards implicit in the concept of the fictional reader of an *epistolary* novel become evident when we pause to reflect on the special format of a letter-novel and on the particular problems posed by such a collection of discrete units inside the single unit that is the novel itself. Susan Lanser presents the part of the problem that involves the narrator in these words:

> In most texts this poses no problem, but difficulties arise when the main text is reported to us by another narrator, usually an editor-figure. This is the case with epistolary novels like *Les Liaisons dangereuses* and memoirs like *Moll Flanders* and *Adolphe*. In these cases, if the letters and the memoirs respectively constitute the primary narrative, with what language can we describe the narrative in which an editor-voice explains that he or she has discovered this material and is passing it along to us? I would call these figures the extradiegetic narrators, and consider the letters or memoir to be an intradiegetic text, but Genette does not.[7]

Just as the epistolary novel's narrator(s) demand(s) special consideration, so too does the fictional reader or listener who exists in symmetrical opposition to the narrator(s). The relatively simple paradigm that Jakobson's communication model produces when applied to an ordinary, third person / omniscient format risks becoming a terribly complex, multi-layered, uncentered series of separate communicative acts in an epistolary novel.

Except for the rare and extreme case of what Jean Rousset[8] calls *la monodie épistolaire* (that is, a one-sided correspondence with no replies as in the case of the *Lettres portugaises* or Crébillon's *Lettres de la Marquise*), the epistolary novel supposes, inside the text, within the fictional world of its correspondents, by the very fact that they write to each other and read each other's letters, an alternation of emitting and receiving, of writing and reading. After writing a letter and thus temporarily functioning as narrator for that single letter, a fictional character may then be called upon to receive another's letter and to read it, thereby becoming, also temporarily, a fictional reader. This necessary alternation between the two narrative poles distinguishes the letter-novel from other formats. Only in an epistolary novel can the same personage participate in this double fashion. To speak then of readers in a letter-novel poses some complex problems: the twin functions of narrator and reader are closely intertwined; each character can perform both functions, but only temporarily and intermittently, for the duration of a single letter at a time; there are numerous readers, just as there are many narrators, and each one is distinctive. Trying to locate "a" single addressee for a polyphonic letter-novel like the *Liaisons dangereuses* is therefore impossible. A more profitable task would be to track down these various addressees and to see how their role as fictional readers and receivers of letters inside the novel, which is to say their reading activity created by Laclos within his fiction, enriches our comprehension of the novel as a whole.[9]

Editeur, Rédacteur, and Mme de Rosemonde

The modern notion of narrator and narrative point of view is relatively easy to fit into eighteenth-century novelistic practice. This is especially true of the *Liaisons dangereuses*, where a certain amount of critical and scholarly attention has been paid to the presence of two editors, one called *l'éditeur*, the other *le rédacteur*, who contradict each other on the nature of the text they are presenting.[10] Their existence within the novel seems to serve no purpose other than to draw our attention to the issue that divides them. Their mutually nullifying prefaces rehearse the traditional debate about the authenticity or the fictionality of the text they introduce. By 1782 this question was moot since the novel had already succeeded in establishing itself as an accepted genre. The authenticating devices used earlier in the century for "true" memoirs and for "real" and "actual" letters were now understood, at least by sophisticated readers, to be simply literary conventions. Seeing through these guises, of course, did not eliminate them entirely: witness Hawthorne's similar efforts[11] as late as 1849 to provide an authentic source for *The Scarlet Letter*. Furthermore, such devices were also a response to the new credibility, not to say naiveté, among the increasing numbers of sentimental readers in the second half of the century who felt that the fictional characters they were reading about must be real. Popular reaction to Rousseau's *La Nouvelle Héloïse* and to Goethe's *Werther* points clearly to such sentimental reading[12] and thus highlights the tension between the novel's (at least half-avowed) fictionality and the impression it intentionally gives of being or at least seeming to be true.

If we smile at thinking that so transparent a device as this pair of editors could cause any confusion, we should reconsider because such errors are not only comprehensible but they continue to this day. To cite only two examples, we can remember that it was only recently that Frédéric Deloffre finally proved that the *Lettres portugaises* was indeed a work of fiction and not the real letters of an amorous nun.[13] In addition, as Georges Roth has shown,[14] Mme d'Epinay's narrative *Histoire de Madame de Montbrillant* is more fiction and novel than memoirs or autobiography. Nonetheless, Elisabeth Badinter uses these *Pseudo-Mémoires* as a document for re-creating and describing Mme d'Epinay's personal thoughts and reactions in her best-selling biography[15] *Emilie, Emilie.*

The nature of truth and fiction, at least in literature, is not always easy to determine, as these examples demonstrate. As for the *Liaisons*, part of the difficulty can be traced back to the presence of those two editors and the nature of their narrative contribution. We would be committing a serious error, one that the epistolary novel's format seems to eschew, if we tried to suppose that the *éditeur* and the *rédacteur* somehow control or "narrate" (in the strictest sense of that term) the letters written by the other characters in the novel except in certain obvious and clearly delineated instances. Even if we have trouble in distinguishing them as extradiegetic or intradiegetic, or in finding the proper language to discuss them (cf. Susan Lanser's comments in the passage quoted above), we have no difficulty in understanding that they belong to the same general fictional universe as do the other characters and that they function within the text according to the author's intentions. Given then their fictional status, we should ask ourselves what fictional purpose they serve: why are they present and why do they contradict each other?

As collector(s), arranger(s), and preparer(s) of the final text of these letters in a number of ways, some specified in notes, others passed over in silence, these two characters play a formal and structural role which, while it does intrude upon these correspondences, cannot be confused with the actual narrating done by the letter writers themselves. Unlike other types of novel, which are dominated by a single narrative voice (even if secondary narrators do exist, in *tiroirs*, for example), the epistolary novel has many voices. These voices are contained in the letters, which are whole, complete, and self-contained in relation to themselves but which are nonetheless fragmentary and partial in relation to the entire novel. No single letter encompasses the whole novel; no letter can erase another one. Every epistolary novel exists in a permanent present tense of the narrative act so that no narrator can interfere with another narrator's narration. However, letters by different narrators must be arranged, and this is done according to some system or logic, usually chronological. The "narrative" function of the editors is limited to selecting and sequencing, and that is quite different from actual narration. An epistolary novel becomes one harmonious whole even though its components, the heterogeneous letters which may contradict or complement each other, always remain discrete and unmixed.

Laclos's *éditeur* and *rédacteur* exist, then, on the fringes of the narrative exchange between the writers and the readers of the novel's letters. They have one foot inside the novel, since they do arrange the sequence of letters, select which ones to publish, and provide a few notes. Their other foot is outside the fiction, since they can be and indeed have been considered an implied author as they mimick the authorial functions of Laclos himself. Without wanting to pronounce on the issue of which one is "right"[16] in this debate over the fictional status of the novel, we can point nonetheless to this ludic incorporation of the question of literary conventions and their validity into the novel itself as one proof that Laclos does understand fully the complexities of the narrative focus he is creating.

Introduction 5

But even if Laclos recognizes the intricacies of the narrator's point of view, is he also aware of the fictional reader within the novel to whom these letters are addressed? By way of reply, let us look at two examples of internal evidence: the first is provided by one of the novel's admittedly minor characters, Mme de Rosemonde; the second by letter 161.

Mme de Rosemonde is the aunt of the Vicomte de Valmont and the proprietor of the château in which much of the action concerning Valmont's seductions of Mme de Tourvel and Cécile Volanges takes place. She participates in the narrative action by writing nine letters herself and receiving twenty-two others. To be more accurate, we should say that Mme de Rosemonde narrates nine letters but she does not write them all. Since she is old and suffers from arthritis, her maid, Adélaide, serves as amanuensis and signs one letter (number 112) which Mme de Rosemonde dictates. This detail might seem insignificant at first glance and unworthy of further attention. But Laclos pays heed to such minute effects and rarely uses them without some larger purpose in mind. This variation on the narrator's usual mode of production (here writing is reduced to speaking or dictating) is not intended merely as an effort to increase verisimilitude, to bring external reality (arthritis and old age) more concretely into the novel, or to heighten the fiction's referential hold (aristocratic privilege, the status of domestics) on the outside world. In addition to all that, Laclos is playing (in the serious sense of the term) with narrative technique by differentiating, individualizing, and varying the narrator's writing or narrating activity and the novel's depiction of it.

While Mme de Rosemonde writes only nine letters, she receives twenty-two which are addressed and sent directly to her. Her role as a listener and a reader would seem then to be more important than her function as a writer. In addition to those addressed to her, she acquires, as the novel closes, a number of other letters originally destined for other readers. Following the duel in which he wounds Valmont mortally, Danceny sends Mme de Rosemonde several letters which the dying Vicomte confided to him and which will incriminate the Marquise de Merteuil beyond repair. At the same time he informs Mme de Rosemonde that she will receive, once Valmont's estate has gone through probate, a much more voluminous correspondence entitled *Compte ouvert entre la marquise de Merteuil et le vicomte de Valmont* which contains all the letters of the Marquise to Valmont and copies of Valmont's replies. Later Danceny sends Mme de Rosemonde the letters written to him by Cécile Volanges which he had refused to return to Mme de Volanges on a previous occasion (letter 174). Mme de Rosemonde also receives Mme de Tourvel's *cassette* upon the latter's death. It contains her correspondence with Valmont (letter 165). In taking such pains to indicate how Mme de Rosemonde has become the custodian and depository for all these different correspondences, Laclos is establishing her as a special reader. At the end of the novel, when all is done and nothing can be changed, Mme de Rosemonde alone can begin to put together all the scattered pieces of these interconnected and yet separate exchanges. Alone of all the personages inside the novel, she can read these crisscrossing correspondences whose very authors were frequently ignorant of their intersections and which, taken together, will comprise the novel we are reading entitled *Les Liaisons dangereuses*.

Those two editors whom we have already mentioned draw our attention to Mme de Rosemonde's growing importance and special status as a reader in one of their notes:

> C'est de cette correspondance, de celle remise pareillement à la mort de Mme de Tourvel, et des lettres confiées aussi à Mme de Rosemonde par Mme de Volanges, qu'on a formé le présent recueil, dont les originaux subsistent entre les mains des héritiers de Mme de Rosemonde. (Letter 169, note, p. 382)[17]

As an actor, Mme de Rosemonde is not a major figure; rather, she is what in the theater would be called a "function," accompanying the more important characters and giving them the pretext to reveal themselves in dialogues or confrontations with her. Nonetheless, she is most important as the ultimate fictional reader who alone can follow all the intrigues, the only imaginary reader who holds all the threads that will be woven into the final fabric, the same novel that we ourselves are reading. Her role as reader within the fiction has been enlarged to make her potentially the first "real" reader outside the novel as well. Her ambiguous position astride the thin line separating the real from the fictitious recalls not only the similarly double situation of the twin editors but also the subject of their disagreement, the authentic vs. the fictional. Mme de Rosemonde and the editors share a similarity of roles and a certain symmetry in their activities as readers and writers caught in the penumbra between real existence and purely fictional status. The playfulness we have noted in the ludic confrontation of the two editors joins the ambiguity of Mme de Rosemonde's declared intention (in letter 171) not to publish what has in fact been published. Of course, since this novel is a fiction, the final mystery of the exact provenance of these letters really has no meaning. But the play, the ludic element, is doubled, just as the editors are double and just as the double function of narrator and reader participates in this circular movement, the end of the novel explaining the beginning, the last fictional reader on the point of becoming the first real or extradiegetic reader, Mme de Rosemonde receiving and collecting these letters that the editors will publish and footnote.

Letter 161 is another bit of evidence which points to a sharp awareness of the role of the fictional reader. This is Mme de Tourvel's last letter and she writes it to . . . no one in particular and everyone in general. The Présidente does not actually write this letter; like Mme de Rosemonde in the previous example, she dictates it to her servant. This letter marks the nearly total disintegration of Mme de Tourvel after she has learned the full extent of Valmont's duplicity. She is dying, distraught and depressed; conscious of her own sin and the moral solitude her weakness has caused, she is going mad. Mad with grief, mad with despair, mad with or because of love, but nonetheless mad. Nothing translates her loss of mental and spiritual equilibrium better than that loss of a specific reader to whom she is addressing her letter. By turns using *tu* and *vous*, she seems to talk to her husband, to Valmont, to her friends like Mmes de Rosemonde and Volanges. This letter hangs suspended in an unreal world of unattached meanings; it is a series of directionless statements and incoherent phrases; it does not make sense because it lacks an explicit recipient to help moor it fast to some intelligible meaning, just as the Présidente floats freely, both physically and spiritually, in something like a semi-coma. The loss of a known and defined reader is then somewhat akin to the loss of consciousness, the loss of one's bearings. This letter is doubtless the single most dramatic illustration of the importance of the fictional reader whose silent and easily overlooked presence remains nonetheless crucial in giving each letter its full significance.

The discussion of Mme de Rosemonde or of the absent addressee in letter 161 will not offer irrefutable proof that Laclos had in mind the same conception of the fictional reader as we do. Nonetheless, the evidence is strong enough to suggest that he was very conscious of the importance of reading by the personages in his novel. Recent scholarship has shown that eighteenth-century novelists exploited the richness of various types of narrators and narrative viewpoints even though they did not formulate as coherent and as comprehensive a theory of narrative as modern novelists and critics have done.[18] Even without a clearly articulated theory of the fictionalized reader, Laclos was more than capable of exploiting the possibilities inherent in the act of reading.

The Postal System: Privileging the Addressee

Having made an effort to establish an awareness of the reader within the novel in terms of its own practice, we now turn to contemporary phenomena outside the realm of literature in our search for examples to bolster our contention that Laclos and other eighteenth-century novelists were not unaware of the importance of readers and of the special significance of the act of reading in an epistolary novel.

Like the memoir-novel, the letter-novel imitated the real life activity that provided its format. In terms of style and content, novelists tried to approximate what normal letters might be.[19] Furthermore, it is not impossible that the very nature of contemporary postal services might furnish us with an insight into the practical value of the reader or the addressee as the latter was perceived by those who did write, read, and exchange real letters during the eighteenth century.

During the same time span when the epistolary novel was a popular and much used form of the genre, the public postal service had not yet become the institution it is today and some of the practices we accept as normal were not yet known. The *timbre-poste,* as we use it today for example, was only introduced to France in 1849. Under the *ancien régime* the recipient of a letter, not the author, paid the cost of its delivery or its *port.*

> Ajoutons dans le domaine des faits que le destinataire payait les taxes postales, rarement l'expéditeur, état de choses que l'administration estime avantageux pour tous.[20]

According to eighteenth-century postal authorities the idea of requiring the addresser rather than the addressee to pay the costs of delivery did not make much sense. They saw that option as a positive impediment to the effective functioning of the postal system:

> La nécessité de l'affranchissement, écrit-elle [i.e., l'administration] dans un document de 1751, est "toujours nuisible à la correspondance des lettres, ce que l'on ne peut contester."[21]

Hand-delivered letters by personal couriers were similar to the public post in that the messenger was frequently offered some financial gratification by the recipient. Thus, in those most practical and significant of terms, financial ones, the intended reader, the recipient, the receiver of a letter, occupied a most critical position in any epistolary exchange. By accepting the letter and consequently paying for it, the reader enabled the whole communication chain to function. Without the reader and his payment, the connection would be broken because the letter would not be delivered.

> Un arrêt du Conseil d'Etat de janvier 1735 . . . faisait défense de remettre aucunes lettres ni paquets à ceux qui avaient précédemment refusé de payer le port d'envois précédents. . . . La sanction était rigoureuse et elle équivalait en somme à l'obligation pour chacun de payer le port des lettres à lui présentées, sous peine de se trouver désormais privé de toute correspondance.[22]

Marked in the most considerable of bourgeois values, money,[23] the act of reception can be considered the defining and the enabling act of any epistolary exchange. No novelist could remain unaware of the practical importance of the reader/receiver, especially novelists whose epistolary fictions mimicked the postal realities all their readers knew at first hand. Anyone could be a narrator, writing and sending letters. He truly existed however only when a reader validated his narrative act by accepting his letter and paying for it. If the reader ever decided to stop receiving and paying, the exchange would be terminated as provided for in the edict of 1735. For us, today, the narrator's emission seems the most important element in the epistolary exchange. But for the eighteenth century, that was not necessarily the case. It was primarily the addressee, the intended reader, who permitted a correspondence to exist, and thus the novel to imitate it, both by his presence and by his purse.

Reading: The Power of the Word

To emphasize and to privilege the imaginary reader at the expense of so many other valid critical approaches is doubtless a dangerous prospect. The intradiegetic or fictionalized reader is, after all, only one element in a complex and many faceted work like the *Liaisons dangereuses*. Other viewpoints and perspectives are certainly equally worthy of study. For us, however, this fictional reader has the virtue of neglect: it has not received much scholarly notice in the many fine works of criticism that have been devoted to Laclos's novel.[24] Breaking new ground and opening up this much appreciated novel to different and perhaps controversial interpretations are certainly factors that justify our exclusive concentration on this single feature. One further advantage is that focusing on the reader allows us to attempt a closed and self-referential study of the novel. By concentrating on the narrative techniques evidenced in this reader, we can deal with this novel as a discourse whose meaning (or, rather, one of whose meanings) is irrevocably bound up in the way it functions as a self-regulating system, a text whose structure and construction are vital parts of its content and significance.

One basic premise to which we will return constantly in analyzing the fictional reader is that the word itself possesses power, speaking is a strategy, and writing a paradox that simultaneously conceals and reveals. This precondition is ideally suited to the epistolary novel whose very format embodies the act of writing, and most especially to the *Liaisons dangereuses,* which combines a sophisticated comprehension of the technical power of the word with a subject matter redolent of strategies and paradoxes. Jean-Luc Seylaz has analyzed the *Liaisons* from a different perspective, but he too emphasizes the fundamental importance of the actual words of the text. In one place he writes:

> ces lettres sont des moyens de combat et des actes. En d'autres termes, elles sont la matière de l'action, et non pas seulement son reflet.

He follows through on this insight later by saying:

> il est, nous l'avons vu, un véritable roman par lettres et . . . les lettres y sont autant un moyen d'action qu'un procédé de narration.[25]

In both the real and the symbolic sense, the action of the *Liaisons* is writing letters, which is to say, giving the phrase an ontological twist, that writing is its own subject. Letters of the alphabet do not merely constitute words of power. Letters of the alphabet also constitute the letters of this letter-novel. They do not merely recount stories of seduction but are themselves the very means and operators of these seductions. Words and the letters they compose are fully active. They are action. Letters in an epistolary novel recount and reenact simultaneously, without distinction. Doing and telling are congruent, interchangeable, identical activities. The Marquise de Merteuil and the Vicomte de Valmont are the principal characters in this novel because they know best how to use the word. They control and direct others through their writing. From our perspective, however, to listen well is an even more critical and fundamental activity than writing well. To receive a letter correctly is similar to capturing its message. In French the technical sense of *capter* is to receive a television or radio signal. The ultimate victor in this novel of seduction and deception, of immoral behavior and perverted intentions, is not necessarily the one who writes best but rather he, or she, who reads best. Both these narrative activities are important, of course, since they are interdependent and complementary. Concentrating on the reader, however, places the entire epistolary exchange in a new light and accentuates the use of the word as an instrument of power and the letter as a tool for domination.

2

A Theory of Fictional Readers and Their Reading

In beginning our analysis, we should recognize that Laclos has scattered a number of reflections on the reading process throughout the one hundred seventy-five letters of his novel and among its fourteen different fictional writers and readers. Articulated by the narrators or the writers of these fictional letters, these comments constitute a theoretical presentation as well as a practical illustration of the nature and purpose of their opposites and counterparts, the fictional readers.

There are five differing aspects to this reading activity. The first touches on the question of narrative awareness, of writing directed at one specific reader who is clearly imagined by the writer, while the second deals with the bond of confidence that links writer and reader. The next element is double, combining the related activities of receiving and responding. The fourth component speaks to the dangers of being a reader: reading can never be an entirely innocent activity in this novel of seduction and deception told through the multiple and deforming prisms of diverse and subjective narrators. Finally, this notion of danger leads inevitably, given the essential role that writing must play in any epistolary novel, to an analysis of the concept of writing as the ultimate libertine act. These five moments in the reading activity are not separate and discrete, however. Rather they are closely interrelated, each one reinforcing the others. Indeed the problem here is to separate and to distinguish them sufficiently so as to be able to discuss them effectively. At this point, criticism does falsify the complete and holistic nature of the novel, a fact which we can bemoan but not alter. Ultimately, this list should suggest an ascending order of components, a gathering of forces pushing towards a climax. Nonetheless, even as the terms employed suggest, the first element, style, or awareness of the reader, is irrevocably implicated in the last, writing.

Awareness of the Reader

Right at the beginning of the novel, the Marquise de Merteuil takes the young Cécile Volanges under her wing and befriends the young girl who, fresh from her convent school, is lost and bewildered in the sophisticated salons of Parisian society. Although Mme de Merteuil is actually using Cécile to avenge herself upon the Comte de Gercourt, Cécile's fiancé, she gives the appearance of helping her make the difficult transition from child to adult. Indeed she even acts like a surrogate mother on occasion. In letter 105, she gives Cécile, who is a most naive and unskilled letter writer, some significant advice about readers. Cécile should keep firmly in mind the person to whom and for whom she is writing:

> quand vous écrivez à quelqu'un, c'est pour lui et non pas pour vous: vous devez donc moins chercher à lui dire ce que vous pensez, que ce qui lui plaît davantage. (Letter 105, p. 247)

Those two prepositions, *for* and *to,* are not redundant because they hint at an important distinction between the apparent and the hidden readers that any letter may have, a phenomenon which we will discuss later and one which Merteuil exploits to the fullest in her own reading and writing. Since the Marquise is referring to Cécile's love letters to Danceny, these notions of pleasing the reader and adopting the appropriate style belong to an amorous as well as to a literary code. In love as in letters, one partner, the narrator, should aim his or her discourse towards what the other, the reader or the addressee, desires or expects. A love letter does not reveal new emotions as much as it confirms those that already exist. It assures and reassures the recipient more than it informs him. Cajoling the reader is thus more important than speaking the truth:

> A propos, j'oubliais... un mot encore. Voyez donc à soigner davantage votre style. Vous écrivez toujours comme un enfant. Je vois bien d'où cela vient; c'est que vous dites tout ce que vous pensez, et rien de ce que vous ne pensez pas. (Letter 105, p. 247, ellipsis in original)

Cécile is a child, while the Marquise is a mature, sophisticated, and intelligent woman of the world, who knows how to best intrigue for her own advantage. The former can only be honest and straightforward, the latter knows too well how to be deceptive. In Merteuil's own words, Cécile is a "petite sotte" who might become "plus raisonnable" if she follows the Marquise's advice.

Mme de Merteuil gives this same lesson on style, albeit in different terms, to Valmont after reading one of his letters to Mme de Tourvel. With him as with Cécile, she finds that the writer's style is not appropriate to the task at hand:

> De plus, une remarque que je m'étonne que vous n'ayez pas faite, c'est qu'il n'y a rien de si difficile, en amour, que d'écrire ce qu'on ne sent pas. Je dis écrire d'une façon vraisemblable: ce n'est pas qu'on ne se serve des mêmes mots; mais on ne

les arrange pas de même, ou plutôt on les arrange, et cela suffit. Relisez votre lettre; il y règne un ordre qui vous décèle à chaque phrase. (Letter 33, p. 67)

In Valmont's letter as in Cécile's, what counts for the Marquise is the impression that the letter leaves with its reader, that is to say, the impact it produces on its recipient through its tone and other intangible elements. In short, Merteuil is talking about its almost indefinable style. The truth can, indeed, it should, be eclipsed by appropriately soothing but nonetheless false words.

Writing is dominated, according to the Marquise de Merteuil, not by external considerations like truth, reality, or the "facts" of a situation, but rather by internal factors and most especially by its intended audience. Merteuil is dreaming of an entirely self-referential and self-conscious discourse, divorced from extradiegetic concerns and focused narrowly on the communicative (or narrative) channel connecting emission and reception. The example she uses to illustrate Valmont's flaw is a literary one, and it thus underlines the purely literary connotations of all these reflections on style and audience. What she criticizes as the Vicomte's *invraisemblable* style,

[c]'est le défaut des romans; l'auteur se bat les flancs pour s'échauffer, et le lecteur reste froid. (Letter 33, p. 67)

Valmont is not however always as unaware of his reader as the Marquise's criticisms might lead us to believe. On occasion he can show himself to be masterful in knowing who his reader is and how that reader will react to what he reads.

Letter 117 is sent by Cécile to Danceny; its purpose is, in the words of another character, to "nourrir l'amour du jeune homme, par un espoir plus certain" (letter 115, p. 275). What is significant from our perspective is that Valmont is the real author of this letter which he has dictated to Cécile, as he himself explains to the Marquise:

je l'ai décidée [Cécile] à en écrire une autre sous ma dictée . . . imitant du mieux que j'ai pu son petit radotage. (Letter 115, p. 275)

Valmont is perfectly aware of who his reader is (Danceny) and of how he, speaking for Cécile, should speak to him. Even more effective from the reader's viewpoint is a subsequent letter again dictated to Cécile by Valmont and again intended for Danceny. In this letter (156) Valmont becomes more enticing, more suggestive, and more seductive in the words he puts into Cécile's mouth and into Danceny's ear, as it were. Not only does "Cécile" tell the Chevalier how to sneak into her room, but she spices this information with "her" own transparent intentions:

> j'espérais que vous essaieriez de profiter de ce temps de liberté. . . . pourquoi donc le cœur me bat-il si fort en vous écrivant? (Letter 156, pp. 362-63)

The Vicomte understands Danceny quite well and knows how he will react to "Cécile's" invitation/temptation. Just as Valmont hoped, Danceny breaks his previous engagement with Mme de Merteuil. Without warning he does not appear at her secret love nest as expected. To the Marquise, Valmont brags about this "ouvrage de mon zèle" (letter 158) even as he jokingly minimizes his own cleverness in directing the Chevalier's actions:

> Au fait, que m'en a-t-il coûté? un léger sacrifice, et quelque peu d'adresse. . . . La lettre que la jeune personne lui a écrite, c'est bien moi qui l'ai dictée. . . . il faut dire la vérité, il n'a pas balancé un moment. (Letter 158, p. 366)

Valmont downplays his skill but only to accentuate it. Both letters, 117 and 156, were written by the Vicomte although he hides as narrator behind Cécile's signature; both reveal him at work like a master puppeteer perfectly cognizant of which strings to pull in order to produce the desired gesture in his reader who throughout remains unaware of this manipulation. Given that Valmont can be so attuned to his reader's emotional state, even his outrageous and sexually ambivalent insult of the Chevalier rings true:

> J'aurai été à la fois son ami, son confident, son rival et sa maîtresse! (Letter 115, p. 275)

These few examples suffice to show how easily truth can be sacrificed to the letter's desire to convince its reader. Merteuil's dishonest advice to Cécile and Valmont's manipulation of his reader prepare us for a novel of and about deceptions, where sexual seduction and licentious conduct depend on mistaken intentions, false emotional displays, and duplicitous appearances. When a narrator like Valmont attacks his reader and victim, Mme de Tourvel, through his letters to her, the simple fact of being a reader is a most critical structural function. By definition, the reader reads. But what is in appearance so simple hides a double reality. The act of reading is profoundly ambiguous and troubling like so many other actions in this novel: the reader can be a friend and confidant or he (and she) can be an interloper and spy. The first type of reader offers a precious and rare opportunity for honest talk, while the second becomes an enemy waiting for the right moment to launch an attack. The role of reader, then, while holding out the hope of sincere communication and honest, confidential exchanges, can be perverted into its opposite. Most appropriately in this world of false personal relationships, the function of the reader is marked by this need to confide in another, a need which only further highlights the risks of communication. Whether in fact this bond of confidence

Fictional Readers and Their Reading

is eventually broken or not is not yet the question. Before the menace of the unfaithful, deceptive, and spying reader can be felt at its fullest intensity, we must experience the alternative, the brighter side of the coin: the bonds of confidence and friendship that link writer to reader.

The Bonds of Confidence

The need to confide fully in another is so powerful that we should not be surprised to find that the most frequent and the most eloquent statements about the bonds of confidence come from the pens of the two most duplicitous personages in the novel, the Vicomte de Valmont and the Marquise de Merteuil. In an early letter to Valmont, Merteuil gives him a proof of assurance and of shared affection which only a true confidante could imagine. After a mocking description of the Présidente, she chides Valmont for desiring such a woman:

> Qui vous eût dit alors, vous désirerez cette femme?... Allons, vicomte, rougissez vous-même, et revenez à vous. Je vous promets le secret. (Letter 5, p. 15, ellipsis in original)

Her jocular tone and mock incredulity in no way invalidate her deeper bond with Valmont and her ultimate respect for him: "je vous promets le secret." She vows not to betray him even if she does not agree with him or thinks he should undertake a more fitting conquest and a more brilliant enterprise than Mme de Tourvel. That single word *secret* is crucial here as it will be in many other contexts. Secrecy is essential to both these seducers. Without it, the seduction of the Présidente and the debauching of Cécile would be impossible. Furthermore, secrecy is the cement that holds their relationship fast. It is a proof of their intimate connection, of their partnership, of their sharing together. It is quite possible that Merteuil was once and remains throughout the novel deeply in love with Valmont. Her ultimate conflict with him, according to this interpretation, stems from her jealousy over Valmont's falling in love with Mme de Tourvel. Whether the Marquise is or is not a rejected lover desperately destroying the man who has spurned her, like Hermione in Racine's *Andromaque*, remains too large a question to answer definitively one way or the other. Any such single interpretation would impoverish this extremely rich and complex novel. Nonetheless, focusing on the reader and his or her need for sharing confidences illuminates one aspect of this question. Reformulating the situation from the perspective of the reader and her emotional needs provides an additional explanation for what we could consider Merteuil's deep, passionate, and insuperable love for the Vicomte.

To keep another's secret, to maintain the other's confidence, and to share a mutual respect with someone else are all actions that fall within the reader's purview. This close connection between keeping secrets and enjoying a very special emotional intimacy informs Merteuil's admission that

> A la vérité, je vous ai depuis livré tous mes secrets: mais vous savez quels intérêts nous unissent, et si, de nous deux, c'est moi qu'on doit taxer d'imprudence. (Letter 81, p. 180)

Merteuil and Valmont are equals and mutual confidants because they have revealed their secrets to each other. By confessing to one another (an interesting libertine variation on the Catholic Church's sacrament of confession) they have created the bonds that hold them together. Given the novel's denouement, the Marquise's smug phrase, which teeters between accusing Valmont of imprudence and praising her own command of the situation, might seem to smack of hubris. We should understand it in its pertinent context, however. It is not at all foolish, rather it is imperative, to establish this confidential link even if it is at the heavy price of confessing one's hidden sins and secrets.

It is interesting to note in passing that Merteuil's need for a confidant goes beyond what even Valmont can provide. Although she undertakes the project to debauch Cécile in part to exact revenge upon Gercourt, another motive is her desire to have a female companion in whom she can confide. Once Cécile is fully debauched and corrupted, she will become the Marquise's friend and confidante, perhaps not her equal but surely someone capable of receiving her secrets:

> je m'attache sincèrement à elle. Je lui ai promis de la former, et je crois que je lui tiendrai parole. Je me suis souvent aperçue du besoin d'avoir une femme dans ma confidence, et j'aimerais mieux celle-là qu'une autre. (Letter 54, pp. 111-12)

Even though she remains the most secretive and duplicitous character in the novel, the Marquise yearns for the transparency that only truly confidential relationships can provide. That plural is essential: alone Valmont cannot entirely fulfill Merteuil's need. This exemplar of deception requires more of the love that confidence provides than Valmont affords her. Ironically, the character who proves to be the least confidential exhibits the greatest need of that virtue.

Each time that Valmont and Merteuil write to each other, they reinforce these bonds. Of course in such an epistolary exchange the narrator who writes is important. But an exchange is a two-way street: to write a letter implies that someone else will read it. Furthermore, in order to maintain any such exchange, the writer must become on occasion a reader, too. From the perspective of confidence, the reader is more significant because he or she continues the exchange: the reader validates the writer's offer of mutual affection and shared secrets by accepting his or her letters and by responding to them in turn. The tragic irony of Valmont and Merteuil's friendship and confidentiality, not to say their love, is felt through the reader and not through the narrator since it is, in both cases, the reader who will betray the writer. Thus it is Mme de Merteuil who reveals Valmont's libertine intentions to the Présidente and informs her indirectly that the Vicomte's love for her is in fact mere physical desire, lust, and *goût*. To break off their relation, Valmont sends Mme de Tourvel a letter (number 141) which proves he never loved her. But this letter was composed by the Marquise and reveals what Valmont had shared with her in confidence. Because she exposes his hidden truth and breaks her promise to keep his secret, Merteuil herself destroys the bonds of confidence that once linked her so closely to the Vicomte. The Vicomte does have his moment of revenge, however, since he has been the Marquise's confidant and special reader just as she was his. By revealing her secret and betraying his faith with her as her reader, he precipitates her downfall. He gives to Danceny letters he has received from the Marquise. He violates his pact of confidence with her, he betrays her trust in him by permitting her secrets to become public, a revelation which ruins her reputation. What causes Valmont's fatal duel with Danceny is another violation of the reader's pact whose cardinal principle is to protect the other's secret and to encourage mutual confidentiality: the Marquise shows Danceny the letters in which Valmont describes his debauching of Cécile. Immediately the Chevalier challenges Valmont to a duel that will prove mortal to the latter.

We have in a sense gotten ahead of ourselves here, speaking of the break-up of Valmont and Merteuil before we have fully documented the extent to which they do share an intimately confidential relationship. Knowing the final resolution of their liaison does not in any way invalidate the strong ties that did once link them. On the contrary, this ultimate reversal points out even more how imperative the need for an authentic and honest reader/sharer/confidant is. Otherwise it is impossible to conceive how two such intelligent and aware individuals would confide such potentially devastating information to anyone. Even though the risk is enormous, the reader elicits the sharing of confidences. The pleasure of having a reader and of being read justifies the danger both these characters risk as writers in so baring their souls. Critics have puzzled over what they consider such foolish behavior on the part of two such clever individuals as Valmont and Merteuil, and consider this confiding in one another a flaw in Laclos's psychological portrait:

> Par contre, sous l'apparente cohérence que projette sur elle la rigoureuse géométrie de la forme épistolaire, si magistralement exploitée par Laclos, la conduite de la marquise reste jusqu'au bout un chef d'œuvre d'invraisemblance.[1]

Proper emphasis on the reader as confidant, however, shows that entrusting one's secrets to a reader who can be a friend and/or lover is emotionally and logically sound. Within the bonds of confidence they create for each other as mutual readers, even such aloof and suspicious individuals as Valmont and Merteuil cannot avoid giving each other the dangerous information that will be the undoing of them both.

Despite their eventual falling-out, these two consummate and careful libertines feel the deep need to experience one sincere, open, frank, and equal communication. Described thus, with such emotion-laden adjectives, their mutual desire for confidence and sharing is indeed just a heartbeat away from being a deep and genuine love. This possibility is not lost on Mme de Tourvel. On the brink of falling hopelessly in love with the Vicomte herself, the Présidente instinctively recognizes how closely those bonds of confidence which tie him to the Marquise resemble the chains of love:

> Sa conduite avec Mme de Merteuil en est une preuve. Il nous en parle beaucoup; et c'est toujours avec tant d'éloges et l'air d'un attachement si vrai, que j'ai cru, jusqu'à la réception de votre lettre, que ce qu'il appelait amitié entr'eux deux était bien réellement de l'amour. (Letter 11, p. 30)

For Valmont and Merteuil, *amitié* takes the form of sharing confidences, an intimate communication that closely resembles love. The actual physical lovemaking Valmont and Merteuil knew before the novel began never (re)appears within the novel itself. It is replaced, or perhaps we should say continued, by writing letters and by sharing secrets. The Présidente's mistake is understandable, then.

Although they are both conducting amorous liaisons with other parties while they write to and confide in each other, both the Vicomte and the Marquise privilege their very special communication and the extraordinary intimacy it implies:

> Je m'aperçois qu'il est trois heures du matin, et que j'ai écrit un volume, ayant le projet de n'écrire qu'un mot. Tel est le charme de la confiante amitié: c'est elle qui fait que vous êtes toujours ce que j'aime le mieux. (Letter 10, p. 28)

Valmont expresses their mutual confidence in even stronger terms:

> Dépositaire de tous les secrets de mon cœur, je vais vous confier le plus grand projet qu'un conquérant ait jamais pu former. (Letter 4, p. 13)

Whenever they write to each other, Valmont and Merteuil maintain this powerful and most personal rapport of reciprocal confidences, shared secrets, and libertine projects. Despite the immoral content of what they say, how they say it is admirable. By confiding in each other, they endow each other with the powerful status of intimate reader, of the one to whom secrets can and should be told.

When the Vicomte is depressed by his unsuccessful efforts to seduce Mme de Tourvel, he turns for comfort and consolation to his friend and confidante, his reader and "depository of all [his] secrets," Mme de Merteuil. As he closes one letter, he echoes the thoughts she expressed in her phrase "la confiante amitié":

> Adieu, ma belle amie. . . . J'ai éprouvé plus d'une fois combien votre amitié pouvait être utile; je l'éprouve encore en ce moment: car je me sens plus calme depuis que je vous écris: au moins, je parle à quelqu'un qui m'entend, et non aux automates auprès de qui je végète depuis ce matin. (Letter 100, p. 232)

Most important for these two exceptional individuals, the reader is an equal. Since they consciously consider themselves conquerors and military heroes, which is to say extraordinary members of a restricted elite, finding an equal is no easy task. In an epistolary novel, letter writing is more than an excuse for exposition or just another technique for advancing plot. Writing a letter to a reader who is one's equal is also an exercise in self-awareness. Without a reader to confide in, without this intimate listener who shares the writer's projects, without an alter ego to appreciate one's exploits, figures like Valmont and Merteuil would be terribly frustrated. Deprived of a critical opportunity to speak their own truth to a counterpart who alone can truly appreciate their intentions, they would also be one-dimensional and much less fascinating than they are. Only the confidence and equality that the confidential reader evokes could produce such conceited but revealing exclamations from the Marquise:

> ce ne fut qu'après avoir bien concerté mon plan, que je pus trouver deux heures de repos. Tel on nous raconte que le Maréchal de Saxe, après avoir fait les dispositions d'une bataille pour le lendemain, s'endormit d'un sommeil tranquille. (Letter 63, p. 124)

A strikingly similar reflection comes from Valmont:

> Jusque-là, ma belle amie, vous me trouverez, je crois, une pureté de méthode qui vous fera plaisir; et vous verrez que je ne me suis écarté en rien des vrais principes de cette guerre, que nous avons remarqué souvent être si semblable à l'autre. Jugez-moi donc comme Turenne ou Frédéric. . . . mais je crains, à présent, de m'être amolli comme Annibal dans les délices de Capoue. (Letter 125, p. 298)

These comparisons are not mere posturings, they are not exercises in self-aggrandizement. Although writer and reader are equals, they are not identical. The latter prods the former to self-analysis and self-revelation, but at the same time by virtue of being different, forestalls any self-delusion. A reader like the Marquise is frequently critical of Valmont. Their bond of confidence does not exclude negative criticism. On the contrary, the possibility of criticizing and of judging negatively enhances the reader's function as mirror and illumination for the speaking narrator.

As Valmont and Merteuil approach the point of their break-up, they can still evoke the powerful connections that once bound them so indissolubly together. The Vicomte repeats that he is ready to become Merteuil's lover once again,[2] even as he recounts his present seductions to her:

> Ne combattez donc plus l'idée, ou plutôt le sentiment qui vous ramène à moi; et après avoir essayé de tous les plaisirs dans nos courses différentes, jouissons du bonheur de sentir qu'aucun d'eux n'est comparable à celui que nous avions éprouvé et que nous retrouverons plus délicieux encore! (Letter 133, p. 317)

The Marquise is a bit more coy but admits to the same longing:

> Au vrai, vous accepter tel que vous vous montrez aujourd'hui, ce serait vous faire une infidélité réelle. Ce ne serait pas là renouer avec mon ancien amant; ce serait en prendre un nouveau, et qui ne vaut pas l'autre à beaucoup près. Je n'ai pas assez oublié le premier pour m'y tromper ainsi. Le Valmont que j'aimais était charmant. Je veux bien convenir même que je n'ai pas rencontré d'homme plus aimable. Ah! je vous en prie, Vicomte, si vous le retrouvez, amenez-le-moi; celui-là sera toujours bien reçu. (Letter 152, p. 356)

We always think of Valmont and Merteuil as cold and hardened libertines. The softer, more intimate, and *aimable* (the French effectively combines both ideas of love and friendship) side of their personalities is much less known. They are, or at least once were, sincere lovers. To be sure, they have changed. Nonetheless, in passages such as these and in their shared concept of the reader as a true confidant and equal, we can glimpse embers of their dying love. The novel contains only allusions and echoes of it. All that demonstrably remains of this once and distant love which now has perhaps disappeared (the doubt is crucial) is their exchanging letters and confidences, and their choosing each other as intimate readers:

> A présent, ma belle amie, j'en appelle à votre justice, à vos premières bontés pour moi; à la longue et parfaite amitié, à l'entière confiance qui depuis ont encore resserré nos liens: ai-je mérité le ton rigoureux que vous prenez avec moi? (Letter 129, p. 308)

Words like *ma belle amie, amitié*, and *confiance* would ring hollow if we did not have before our eyes the proof of this bond, the very letters they have written to each other, the dangerous secrets they have exchanged, and the intimate, true selves they have revealed only to each other.

The rupture of these former lovers and current master rakes is an element of the plot as important and as weighty as the seduction of Mme de Tourvel and the debauching of Cécile, precisely because there once existed between these two enemies a sincere love, a genuine *amitié,* a real respect and affection. Merteuil herself makes clear this link between love and confidence when she threatens to cease confiding her secrets in Valmont because he has been attracted to a woman whom she detests and whom she regards as a dangerous rival:

> je suis tentée surtout de vous retirer ma confiance. Je ne m'accoutumerai jamais à dire mes secrets à l'amant de Mme de Tourvel. (Letter 5, p. 16)

If Valmont really loves the Présidente, then he prefers her to the Marquise; if she is not first in the Vicomte's affections, Merteuil cannot feel secure as his friend and confidante. Libertine activities and mere sexual conquests have no effect on these bonds. Only another real love, only a sincere outside attachment, can menace them. Ironically, their break-up stems from the same bonds of confidence that made them lovers. As friend, confidant, lover, and reader, each knows too much about the other not to be a most formidable opponent. Being such an intimate reader is not a partial occupation, it involves a total response, be it positive or negative. Thus, when their intimate relationship as mutual readers of each other's letters is broken, they have no choice but to become implacable enemies. As if to highlight this breakdown of communication at the personal level, one single letter also records the parallel deterioration of the reader's confidential status. Strictly speaking, Merteuil does not reply to the letter written by Valmont in which he makes a last plea for reconciliation underlined by a threat they both know is real:

> chacun de nous ayant en main tout ce qu'il faut pour perdre l'autre, nous avons un égal intérêt à nous ménager mutuellement: . . . de ce jour même je serai votre amant, ou votre ennemi. (Letter 153, p. 357)

His plea is in vain. Merteuil does not even bother to write a legitimate letter in reply. For the first and last time, she refuses to be his reader; for once she ceases to be his confidante, the receiver of his secrets as well as of his letters. But once suffices, as Valmont's ultimatum makes perfectly clear. She rejects his communication, she breaks the bond connecting writer and reader. By writing the words "Hé bien! la guerre" at the bottom of his letter, the Marquise not only answers his belligerent demand with an appropriate military metaphor, but she also replicates the content of her message in her gesture. She does not reply with a letter of her own. On the contrary, she thoroughly exploits the deepest significance of the reader's function. She returns Valmont's letter, she refuses to keep it, and thus she annuls his right to speak to her. By writing those words at its end, she transforms his letter into her reply, his question into her answer, his demand of exchange into her refusal to communicate. Thus, in terms of both form and content, she alters their relationship of love and cooperation into one of hatred and animosity. Refusing to keep his letter and to reply with one of her own is a dramatic gesture that violates the very premises of the narrative exchange and that destroys the confidence that had previously united these mutual readers.

Shortly before this emphatic break-down of communication and confidence, there is a clear warning sounded in recognizably similar terms. As the Vicomte and the Marquise exasperate each other with their prickly pride and mutual criticisms, Merteuil suddenly blurts out:

> Mon Dieu! Vicomte, que vous me gênez par votre obstination! Que vous importe mon silence? (Letter 141, p. 331)

Silence is the reader's ultimate weapon, the last resort. Whenever a response is expected, and more pertinently a confidential response, silence and the refusal to reply carry a tremendous significance. The Marquise is not the only character who exploits this "language" of silence to emphasize a meaning. In the novel's closing pages, Mme de Volanges asks Mme de Rosemonde to tell her who was guilty, Danceny or her own daughter, and whether she can still comtemplate Cécile's marriage to Gercourt.

> Vous jugez combien je désire que vous me répondiez, et quel coup affreux me porterait votre silence. (Letter 173, p. 390)

Rosemonde does not reply, however. Silence is here an explicit answer, albeit a cruel and unwelcome one, just as Merteuil's silence with Valmont was a positive declaration. Like Valmont, Mme de Volanges knows how to interpret what silence can say:

> J'espère que vous n'oubliez pas, ma chère amie, que dans ce grand sacrifice que je fais, je n'ai d'autre motif, pour m'y croire obligée, que le silence que vous avez gardé vis à vis de moi. . . . ma fille est donc bien coupable?... Vous pardonnerez sans doute à une mère de ne céder que difficilement à cette affreuse certitude. (Letter 175, p. 394, second ellipsis in original)

Returning to the bonds of confidence, we find that other characters have a similarly strong need for the kind of confidant that only the reader can be. At that desperate point when she realizes she loves Valmont but that her situation as a married woman makes this love unlawful and sinful, Mme de Tourvel asks Mme de Rosemonde to be her confidante, her consolation, and her protector:

Fictional Readers and Their Reading

> Jamais, sans doute, je ne consentirai à rougir à vos yeux, et retenue par ce frein puissant, tandis que je chérirai en vous l'indulgente amie confidente de ma faiblesse, j'y honorerai encore l'ange tutélaire qui me sauvera de la honte. (Letter 102, p. 236)

Alone the Présidente cannot combat her love for Valmont. With the aid of an intimate reader in whom she can confide, however, she hopes to triumph over it. In her loneliness and during this desperate struggle which she fears she is losing, Mme de Tourvel realizes that her salvation lies in becoming a child again and in finding sympathetic maternal consolation. She turns then not to her real mother, but rather to a reader who is more consoling and helpful than any family relation:

> Ah! Madame, pardon: mais mon cœur est oppressé; il a besoin d'épancher sa douleur dans le sein d'une amie également douce et prudente: quel autre que vous pouvait-il choisir? Regardez-moi comme votre enfant. Ayez pour moi les bontés maternelles; je les implore. (Letter 102, p. 235)

At the end of the letter she repeats this same demand in more precise terms:

> aimez-moi comme votre fille, adoptez-moi pour telle. (Letter 102, p. 237)

The bonds of confidence the Présidente seeks are maternal while Valmont and Merteuil prefer an equal and symmetrical relationship. In both cases, readers provide what is required. Mme de Rosemonde responds in moving terms. While denying that as a reader and confidante she might possess any special competence, she does agree to listen to the Présidente's sorrows and to accept her secrets:

> Je ne soulagerai pas vos peines, mais je les partagerai. C'est à ce titre que je recevrai volontiers vos confidences. Je sens que votre cœur doit avoir besoin de s'épancher. Je vous ouvre le mien; l'âge ne l'a pas encore refroidi au point d'être insensible à l'amitié. Vous le trouverez toujours prêt à vous recevoir. Venez avec confiance vous y reposer de vos cruelles agitations. (Letter 103, p. 238)

Even though she denigrates her own value as consolation, Mme de Rosemonde nonetheless understands the emotional impact a reader can have. She listens to the Présidente's sorrows, she opens her heart to friendship, and she realizes that her function as listener/reader is to be the one to whom the Présidente can speak and unburden herself. The proof that the reader can provide the consolation needed in times of tribulation resides in the Présidente's reaction to Mme de Rosemonde's sympathetic response:

> que j'avais besoin de votre lettre! (Letter 108, p. 253)

Most tellingly, Mme de Rosemonde promises not to relieve her pains but rather to share them. It would be difficult to find a more sympathetic or comprehensive definition of the bonds of confidence that comprise one aspect of reading .

Lest we think that the need for a confidant is the exclusive province of women, we should look quickly at the Chevalier Danceny. After Mme de Volanges discovers his correspondence with Cécile and bans him from her house, Danceny feels lost and betrayed. He is in desperate need of someone to talk to, and Valmont easily fills this role as his emotional crutch.

> Je n'ose confier au papier le secret de mes peines: mais j'ai besoin de les répandre dans le sein d'un ami sûr et sensible. (Letter 60, p. 120)

Despite the danger of revealing his secrets (Mme de Volanges just discovered his secret correspondence and his secret love for Cécile), the need to confide in a reader remains permanent and unchangeable.

Finally, Cécile Volanges is another personage who needs a confidant, a reader to whom she can write and speak. In one sense, Danceny will fill this role since he is in love with her and corresponds with her. However, from the perspective of the confidential reader, Mme de Merteuil is a much more interesting choice to study. Right from the beginning of the novel, we know that Cécile is lost in the Parisian social whirl and that her mother is much too preoccupied with arranging a brilliant marriage to look after her daughter properly. The Marquise recognizes this opportunity and exploits Cécile's need for affection to her own disreputable ends. Cécile herself does not recognize the ulterior motives inspiring Merteuil's conduct, as her naive enthusiasm demonstrates:

> Mon Dieu, que vous êtes bonne, Madame! comme vous avez bien senti qu'il me serait plus facile de vous écrire que de vous parler! Aussi, c'est que ce que j'ai à vous dire est bien difficile; mais vous êtes mon amie, n'est-il pas vrai? Oh! oui, ma bien bonne amie! (Letter 27, p. 57)

Cécile's emotional need for a confidante is the same as the Présidente's although not yet as desperate. However, whereas Mme de Tourvel chose the honest and reliable Mme de Rosemonde as her reader, Cécile opens herself to the Marquise, who exploits her confidential status as a reader in order to further her own plans for vengeance against Cécile's fiancé, Gercourt. The culmination of Cécile's misplaced confidence comes after she is debauched by Valmont, whom the Marquise has aided duplicitously:

> Ah! mon Dieu, Madame, que je suis affligée! que je suis malheureuse! Qui me consolera dans ma peine? qui me conseillera dans l'embarras où je me trouve? . . . Il faut que je parle à quelqu'un, et vous êtes la seule à qui je puisse, à qui j'ose me confier. Vous avez tant de bonté pour moi! . . . grondez-moi bien, car je suis

bien coupable: mais après, sauvez-moi; si vous n'avez pas la bonté de me conseiller, je mourrai de chagrin.... Oui, je vous dirai tout. (Letter 97, pp. 218-19)

No other passage expresses the deep emotional need for a reader as well as this one. Cécile clearly sees Merteuil as her consolation and salvation ("sauvez-moi") because the Marquise is willing and able to listen, to play the role of reader: "vous êtes la seule à qui je puisse, à qui j'ose me confier."

Cécile's reader contrasts sharply, then, with Mme de Tourvel's. The latter has found a true confidante, while the former has unwittingly selected as her protector the person who is preparing to sacrifice her to Valmont. The reader as confidant is not a simple phenomenon. Mme de Tourvel's reader is sincere and straightforward, while Cécile's reader perverts the correct function of reading. Just as Merteuil and Valmont will ultimately let their excellent relationship as intimate readers, full of love, confidence, friendship, and sharing, slip and degenerate into implacable hatred, so too is Cécile's trust in Mme de Merteuil a perversion of the genuine affection that binds the Présidente and Mme de Rosemonde. The reader has then at least a double relation to confidence. Since only a reader can vitalize the writer and make him exist, he or she is the sole figure in this novel who can offer the intimacy, the confidentiality, the friendship, and the willing ear that the narrator desires. That possibility, however, does not guarantee its realization. A reader may be true and helpful, like Mme de Rosemonde. On the other hand, a reader may also be deceitful, like the Marquise. One of the most successful achievements of the *Liaisons dangereuses* is this multiplicity, these repetitions ornamented with subtle variations. While not employing a broad range of effects, Laclos does nonetheless constantly modify his repertory so as to produce such a richness and complexity.

Sexual licentiousness, seduction, the debauching of minors, and the violation of marriage vows are all part of the shocking subject matter of the *Liaisons dangereuses,* and part of the reason why this novel, like so many other eighteenth-century *romans libertins,* was placed on the Catholic Church's index of forbidden books and in the *enfers* of French libraries. But even more disquieting and pernicious is the egotistical and self-serving conduct which allows a deceptive reader to betray the most basic social values of trust and confidentiality and even the fundamental literary code of reciprocal exchange which causes him (or her) to exist. In dealing with Cécile, the Marquise has deceived her young confidante and at the same time stripped the very notion of confidence of any meaning. Merteuil's conduct regarding Cécile revolts us because it offends our most fundamental sense of decency. Compounding this offense is the undoubted pleasure that Merteuil finds in being both the cause of misfortune (since she has delivered Cécile to Valmont like a lamb to the slaughter) as well as the consolation of the victim, the final listener to Cécile's tale of woe. Secretly Mme de Merteuil intiates the course of events which is being told to her as if she were a stranger to it all, entirely ignorant of what is happening. This double optic is created by the dishonest reader; it seems especially perverse because it is so incompatible with our normal notions of honesty and confidentiality. At the same time such a dishonest reader is marvelously appropriate to the immoral atmosphere of this licentious novel. A good portion of this novel's moral force and dramatic tension rests precisely on this opposition between the honest reader, the faithful confidant, and the sympathetic listener on one hand; and on the other, the dishonest reader, the false counselor, and the betrayer of secrets.

Receiving and Responding

In our examination of the fictional reader, letters can be aimed directly at a particular addressee and the exchange of letters can indicate a high degree of confidence and trust between the correspondents. That trust can be abused, however, just as the awareness of who a particular reader is can be turned against the best interests of that same reader. Such potential for abuse in the narrative channel connecting reader and writer leads us logically to consider the very basis of the addressee's existence: receiving. To receive a letter or to take delivery of a letter are acts that acknowledge the one who writes the letter; they implicitly accept the validity of this exchange and admit the writer into the reader's private space. To accept a letter is a conscious choice, since to refuse a letter is also a possibility: as we have just seen, Merteuil refused to accept Valmont's letter 153 by returning it with her bellicose postscript added. To receive a letter is then the first step along the path of a relationship that is not entirely innocent; the second step, closely related to the first, is to respond. These two acts, to receive and to respond, define another key function of the imagined reader in any literary discourse and most pertinently in an epistolary novel, since such a novel incorporates into its very format fictional readers and writers.[3] In the *Liaisons dangereuses* Laclos has closely intertwined the subject matter of his novel with its formal, technical realization.[4] Seduction requires two participants, the aggressor and the victim, who must remain in contact or communication with each other. The exchange of letters between Valmont and Mme de Tourvel, for example, is simultaneously part of the problem and part of the solution. A problem for the Présidente, because the letters cause her downfall; a solution for Valmont, since they are the means of his victory. By exchanging letters with the Vicomte, Mme de Tourvel gives him the opening he needs to seduce her. For Valmont, these letters might at first seem a poor substitute for the real sexual pleasure he will eventually enjoy by making love to the Présidente. And yet, in the fictional world of this novel, these letters have a consistency, a texture, and a reality that Valmont's sexual activities, mentioned but never fully described, can simply not rival. On a more libertine level, where the Marquise de Merteuil seems most at home, the letter is felt to be a perfectly adequate vehicle for the intellectual pleasures of seduction and the diabolical enjoyment of such victories of the head rather than those of the heart or of the body. By choosing to write his story of these dangerous love affairs in the epistolary format, Laclos has seized on a literary technique whose own nature and functioning are most compatible with the story he wants to tell. If we conflate plot line and technique, we realize how close the fit between them really is. The reader occupies the most vulnerable position in relation to the seducer. As a reader, he or she listens, and that apparently simple action provides the sole advantage the aggressor requires to press the attack and achieve victory. As writer and initiator of all correspondence, the narrator is perfectly suited to the role of aggressor and attacker. As the receiver of the message, the reader is naturally handicapped by his or her passive situation.

Before continuing this abstract fitting of the reader to his or her position in the war between the sexes, let us look more closely at Mme de Tourvel, who illustrates perfectly the dilemma of being an addressee and who lives out the tragic implications latent in the act of receiving letters.

Valmont is fully cognizant of the danger the Présidente runs in accepting his letters, that is to say, his sexual advances. He is therefore understandably miffed when she refuses to be his reader and tries to escape him by not receiving what he sends her. He explains to the Marquise how she has refused to accept his letters:

> Depuis l'affaire du 19, mon inhumaine, qui se tient sur la défensive, a mis à éviter les rencontres une adresse qui a déconcerté la mienne. . . . Mes lettres mêmes sont le sujet d'une petite guerre: non contente de n'y pas répondre, elle refuse de les recevoir. (Letter 34, p. 69)

The military metaphor is perfectly apt. This "little war" replicates in miniature the war between the sexes that both Valmont and Merteuil are conducting against the rest of humanity. "In miniature" is not quite accurate, however: the fate of a human being hangs in the balance, while the final ramifications of this conflict will visit catastrophe on all the participants in the novel. The connection between letters and sexual activity is never overtly declared but remains implied throughout. The actual physical climax of Valmont's attacks and the physical succumbing of the Présidente remain invisible in the novel, since the perspective provided by letters does not easily record such an incident. What replaces this absent climax then is what the epistolary record provides most naturally: letters themselves. As they exchange letters, Valmont seduces the Présidente by his rhetoric, through his words and letters, which, like his own personality of which they are but reflections, are thoroughly devious and deceptive. Valmont is quite justified then in using this military image. The Présidente has indeed taken a defensive position, which is to say the passive one of refusing her role as reader or receiver. Significantly, he equates actions and words, meetings and letters, and quite possibly privileges the latter. Even if the Présidente succeeds in avoiding Valmont physically, as she does when she flees the château and returns to Paris, she remains vulnerable as long as he can reach out and touch her by letter.

Another reader/victim, Cécile Volanges, is young and unsophisticated, but she understands full well that entering into a correspondence with Danceny is a culpable action:

> Vous étiez si triste, hier, Monsieur, et cela me faisait tant de peine, que je me suis laissée aller à vous promettre de répondre à la lettre que vous m'avez écrite. Je n'en sens pas moins aujourd'hui que je ne le dois pas. (Letter 19, p. 40)

The reader's responsibility for the act of receiving is so strong that Cécile accepts all the blame for her contact with the Chevalier. Moreover, she thinks that she alone is on morally shaky ground when Danceny ought to be just as guilty as she:

> j'espère que vous ne me demanderez pas de vous écrire davantage. J'espère aussi que vous ne direz à personne que je vous ai écrit; parce que sûrement on m'en blâmerait, et que cela pourrait me causer bien du chagrin. J'espère surtout que vous même vous n'en prendrez pas mauvaise idée de moi. (Letter 19, pp. 40-41)

The reader who takes that inevitable second step and responds finds herself in a most compromising position. Cécile has answered Danceny for understandable and forgivable reasons. Yet even honest intentions can lead to dishonest results. After having gone to confession and heard her priest's advice, Cécile pleads with the Chevalier to stop writing her, since she no longer wishes to receive his letters nor to answer them.

> En conséquence, je vous demande d'avoir la complaisance de ne plus m'écrire, d'autant que je vous préviens que je ne vous répondrais plus. (Letter 49, p. 102)

For Cécile the sin she has confessed demands an epistolary penance. Sin and sex stem from the verbs *recevoir* and *répondre*. Both Mme de Tourvel and Cécile realize instinctively that their best resistance, in fact the only way to avoid the sexual consequences of reading and writing, is not to accept those letters in the first place. Thus the Présidente in her very first letter to Valmont expresses the best course of action to follow:

> Hé bien, Monsieur, le silence et l'oubli, voilà les conseils qu'il me convient de vous donner, comme à vous de suivre. (Letter 26, p. 56)

Fictional Readers and Their Reading

Later in the same letter she repeats her desire not to become his reader and consequently his victim even if she does not yet formulate the necessary link between these two terms:

> vous me forceriez à ne vous revoir jamais, si vous ne vous imposiez sur cet objet un silence qu'il me semble avoir droit d'attendre, et même d'exiger de vous. (Letter 26, p. 56)

Mme de Tourvel's tragedy turns on the fact that she cannot act upon her intention *not* to be Valmont's reader. On this point Cécile is luckier than the Présidente: she is responding to a naive but sincere young admirer while Mme de Tourvel is dealing with an accomplished rake determined to undo her. The sincerity of the communication is not under consideration here, nor is the intention of the narrator. Rather we wish to emphasize how this seemingly unimportant matter of receiving letters and responding to them constitutes one of the pivotal elements of the plot and a critical element in the psychological development of the characters.

Not every reader is a victim, like Mme de Tourvel and Cécile, to be sure. Still, their role as victims depends heavily on their role as readers and receivers of letters. If they had never read these letters, they would never have been seduced. This intimate and necessary connection between the roles of reader and victim highlights the key status of the reader as well as the fact that Laclos has once again used a natural or normal aspect of epistolary technique in a manner most effectively adapted to his own novel.

The slippery path on which Cécile has already embarked leads from receiving letters to answering them to another more precise but also more forbidden action. Mme de Tourvel hestitates longer than Cécile. She eventually gives in too, but only with many misgivings, since she knows how easily *écouter* leads to *répondre,* which will ultimately bring her to sin, disgrace, and death. In one letter she argues that she should not even entertain the thought of Valmont and *a fortiori* should not feel the slightest affection for him. She closes this argument about repressing her sexual longings in terms that are also appropriate for describing her situation as a reader:

> je m'en tiens à vous prier, comme je l'avais déjà fait, de ne plus m'entretenir d'un sentiment que je ne dois pas écouter, et auquel je veux encore moins répondre. (Letter 50, p. 104)

The two actions that define the fictional reader's existence, listening and responding, accepting letters and replying to them, are sexually charged for Mme de Tourvel and constitute an essential part of Valmont's seduction of her.

Sending letters is an aggressive maneuver, one part of the Vicomte's libertine attack, while receiving letters, on Mme de Tourvel's part, contributes to her inevitable defeat, just like the woman/citadel besieged in the military metaphor. An epistolary correspondence can then be a battlefield, a military campaign, and a series of victories and defeats that constitute the seduction of a woman. Valmont always has the advantage of being the narrator and writer. Therefore he can initiate new advances despite temporary setbacks, whereas the reader, Mme de Tourvel, is compelled to passive resistance, to a defensive attitude that rebuffs Valmont but that cannot eliminate him:

> Pourquoi vous attacher à mes pas? pourquoi vous obstiner à me suivre? Vos lettres, qui devaient être rares, se succèdent avec rapidité. Elles devaient être sages, et vous ne m'y parlez que de votre fol amour. Vous m'entourez de votre idée, plus que vous ne le faisiez de votre personne. Ecarté sous une forme, vous vous reproduisez sous une autre. (Letter 56, p. 115)

Proteus-like, Valmont adopts differing tactics, diverse words and deeds in order to seduce the Présidente. This ability to change forms, clearly pointed out by the Présidente, confirms our remarks about the continuity of the seductive struggle from letter writing and reading to actual physical consummation. Valmont is not seducing Mme de Tourvel by his good looks, his social rank, or the deference shown to him by others in public. These factors are to be imagined, noted, accepted. But in terms of the novelistic record, all that counts is the text itself, that is, the letters he writes to her. His seduction is epistolary. All that we know of it is contained in those letters; more accurately, it is not in the letters, it *is* the letters. Once again, content and technique join. These epistles, these exchanges between writer and reader, are not just the record of a seduction, they are the seduction itself.[5] Only when we accept this radical definition of letters as the very process, the very stuff, of seduction do we feel all the implications of the Présidente's plea to be left alone:

> Laissez-moi, Monsieur, laissez-moi, ne me voyez plus, ne m'écrivez plus, je vous en prie; je l'exige. Cette lettre est la dernière que vous recevrez de moi. (Letter 56, p. 115)

Mme de Tourvel is not at all mistaken here when she mixes her verbs: to write her equals to see her. Both verbs describe Valmont's invasion of her private space. For Valmont's writing to her is not just a bother or a harassment. On the contrary, his writing is the esesence of his seduction. To break off the correspondence, to refuse to continue to be his reader, is therefore a most extreme action. Indeed it is the only tactic that can protect the Présidente. Her threat that this is the last letter she will write in reply to him is a powerful counterattack, or at least an effective defensive strategy. As long as she conttinues to write him, however, a proposition which supposes that she has already received something from him and that she is replying to it, she remains vulnerable to his attacks.

Unfortunately for Mme de Tourvel, this will not be her last letter to Valmont despite the emphatic tone of her threat. Because their correspondence continues and because she remains his reader, she is condemned to fight off his continued attacks until she finally succumbs to them. Her vulnerability as a reader becomes increasingly apparent as she attempts to justify her contact with the Vicomte, which is constantly prolonged by her cooperation and by her sexually symbolic correspondence with him:

> Je ne voulais plus vous répondre, Monsieur. . . . Cependant je ne veux vous laisser aucun sujet de plainte contre moi; je veux vous convaincre que j'ai fait pour vous tout ce que je pouvais faire. (Letter 67, p. 136)

Mme de Tourvel is attempting to explain away intellectually the emotional need she feels to answer Valmont. Her analysis of the situation is excellent (i.e., she should break off with him), but she is incapable of executing her own project. Here the heart has surely stymied the head. Perhaps there is also a grain of truth in the old expression, wanting "to get the last word in." Whichever answer is the most accurate, her dilemma as reader is evident. Even though any prolongation of their epistolary connection makes her more helpless and Valmont more enterprising, Mme de Tourvel cannot bring herself to stop reading and writing him. Within the same letter she contradicts herself and thwarts her own best interest. She comments:

> votre correspondance a été telle que chacune de vos lettres me faisait un devoir de ne plus vous répondre. (Letter 78, p. 162)

But such an accurate appraisal of the situation does not prevent the Présidente from yielding and continuing their exchange:

> Cependant, comme vous me demandez des éclaircissements, et que, grâces au ciel, je ne sens rien en moi qui puisse m'empêcher de vous les donner, je veux bien entrer encore une fois en explication avec vous. (Letter 78, p. 160)

Of course, Mme de Tourvel has tried to impose some conditions and limitations on her being Valmont's reader and receiver:

> Je vous ai permis de m'écrire, dites-vous? J'en conviens; mais quand vous me rappelez cette permission, croyez-vous que j'oublie à quelles conditions elle vous fut donnée? (Letter 67, p. 136)

She fails, however. Her defense is illusory. The dilemma of the Présidente as well as that of any victimized reader is that she has participated and perhaps even cooperated in her own undoing even though at first she did not fully realize the consequences of reading. The sole condition that allows Valmont to continue his advances is that Mme de Tourvel receive his letters and respond to them. Her threat to stop reading his letters is the most powerful weapon at her disposal, but she fails to use it convincingly or effectively:

> mais je vous préviens que le premier mot d'amour la détruit [her confidence in him] à jamais, et me rend toutes mes craintes; que surtout il deviendra pour moi le signal d'un silence éternel vis-à-vis de vous. (Letter 67, p. 137)

Often repeated, this menace is never enforced. By failing to use the one and only effective weapon she possesses, Mme de Tourvel assures her own defeat. Still, she refuses to recognize her own fault and tries rather to reconcile the culpability of her willingness to be a reader with her innocence:

> Si j'y eusse été aussi fidèle que vous l'avez été peu [to the conditions of their exchange], auriez-vous reçu une seule réponse de moi? Voilà pourtant la troisième; et quand vous faites tout ce qu'il faut pour m'obliger à rompre cette correspondance, c'est moi qui m'occupe des moyens de l'entretenir. (Letter 67, p. 136)

These words are more accurate than the Présidente knows. Ironically she does not realize how essential her own voluntary participation is in their correspondence and consequently in her own seduction and downfall. It is true that she has been wronged by the Vicomte. He often violated their agreement by talking love, but she did not fulfill her part of the bargain, which would have been to break off their correspondence immediately. She is at least partially responsible for her final defeat because she allowed his continued attacks to take place. Her lapidary phrasing and somewhat convoluted syntax (contrary-to-fact clauses symmetrically arranged and articulated by an inverse proportion "aussi fidèle . . . peu") at first hide this implicit admission. Her second phrase is not at all ambiguous, and there the Présidente indicates how important the reader's willing participation in this exchange which brings about her own destruction really is: "c'est moi qui m'occupe des moyens de l'entretenir." Unless the addressee listens and reads, the writer or addresser speaks in vain. Because she was ignorant of (or should we simply and accusingly say: because she ignored) the theory of the fictional reader, Mme de Tourvel foolishly ran the risks that resulted in her own tragic fall.

To exactly the same extent that she continues to be Valmont's reader, willingly accepting his letters and responding to them, Mme de Tourvel compromises the integrity of her own resistance and the strength of her resolve:

> peut-être l'embarras que j'éprouve en ce moment est-il lui-même une preuve qu'en effet je ne le devrais pas [answer him]. (Letter 67, p. 136)

No matter how much she tries to minimize the significance of her choice, there can be no doubt that she is choosing to continue their correspondence and therefore to run the risks involved:

> Qui lirait vos lettres, me croirait injuste et bizarre. Je crois mériter que personne n'ait cette idée de moi. . . . comme, de mon côté, je ne crois pas avoir à y perdre [in discussing and continuing their letter writing], au moins à vos yeux, je ne craindrai pas de m'y livrer. (Letter 78, p. 161)

Lucid as she is, the Présidente sees the contradiction in her own conduct. Yet she continues to write to him and to receive his letters. This inconsistency, which she qualifies merely as "une condescendance peut-être blâmable" (p. 162), will have far-reaching and fatal consequences for her. Even as she writes to say *no* to the idea of loving Valmont, the act of writing is itself another way of saying *yes*. To understand such self-contradiction we must realize that Mme de Tourvel is something of an expert at splitting hairs. She does enjoy Valmont's company, although she does not want this openly acknowledged affection to go too far:

> En vous offrant mon amitié, Monsieur, je vous donne tout ce qui est à moi, tout ce dont je puis disposer. (Letter 67, p. 136)

The slippery path that led from receiving to responding is the same path that leads from *amitié* to *amour*. The thin line separating the two terms is practically invisible and nonexistent. Once engaged on that dangerous slope, the Présidente is lost. All that she controls is her status as a reader, and that she gives fully to Valmont. He requires nothing else to complete this seduction, as he himself warns her in his usual ambiguous but ultimately truthful manner:

> il vous serait plus facile de ne pas lire mes raisons que d'y répondre. (Letter 36, p. 74)

Just as she gives herself to him as a reader, in terms of the literary code, so too will she give herself to him physically and sexually.

It is therefore Valmont himself who best sees and expresses what Mme de Tourvel has promised by becoming his reader and responding to his letters. He fully understands the sexual implications of receiving letters. This is why he wants to "entrer avec elle, et de son aveu, en correspondance réglée" (letter 40, *suite*, p. 87). What is most important, he wants Mme de Tourvel to read and to write him willingly: *de son aveu*. Seduction is not only a physical enterprise for the Vicomte, the mere contact of two epidermises. A complete libertine, he demands also the conscious surrender of his victim, which is more a matter of the mind and will than of the body. His desire is more spiritual (meaning in this context: what involves the mind or spirit) than physical since he demands that Mme de Tourvel accept him willingly. The parallel between the reader accepting letters and the woman accepting her lover subtends Valmont's own explanation of the situation:

> Ce n'est pas assez pour moi de la posséder, je veux qu'elle se livre. Or, il faut pour cela non seulement pénétrer jusqu'à elle, mais y arriver de son aveu; la trouver seule et dans l'intention de m'écouter. (Letter 110, p. 259)

Earlier we saw how *écouter* was a key word in our discussion of the reader who receives letters and responds to them. We have also discussed how Mme de Tourvel accepts Valmont's letters: by listening to his advances, she permits his sexual attacks upon herself. In this passage Valmont's own words confirm the sexual implications of the term *écouter* and of the act of reading. In the libertine context, an epistolary correspondence suggests other tpes of communication or exchanges. To be a reader foreshadows the possibility of becoming a sexual partner. Two aspects of a single reality, each term implies the other. The reader, like a willing sexual partner, allows the other to arrive, to penetrate her. She gives herself to him by listening and reading.

To respond or not to respond is also a question that bedevils Cécile Volanges. After having received one of Danceny's letters, she is eager to answer him, but she knows that this is a serious and compromising step. She seeks advice from the Marquise de Merteuil in words which clearly reveal what she would prefer to do:

> Dites-moi, je vous en prie, Madame, est-ce que ce serait bien mal de lui répondre de temps en temps? . . . Tenez, en lisant sa dernière lettre, j'ai pleuré, que ça ne finissait pas; et je suis bien sûre que si je ne lui réponds pas encore, cela nous fera bien de la peine. (Letter 27, p. 58)

Danceny is reacting melodramatically to Cécile's temporary silence, as befits his as yet unsophisticated personality:

> Eh! quoi, Mademoiselle, vous refusez toujours de me répondre! rien ne peut vous fléchir; et chaque jour emporte avec lui l'espoir qu'il avait amené! (Letter 28, p. 59)

With characteristic hyperbole, he goes on to call her *ingrate* for not replying to his offer of *amitié* which will lead to *un malheur éternel.* He ends on a similar note, emphasizing that key word, *to respond*:

> Je n'ose plus me flatter d'une réponse; l'amour l'eût écrite avec empressement, l'amitié avec plaisir, la pitié même avec complaisance. (Letter 28, p. 60)

When Cécile does finally answer him, he explodes with joy. This reaction is most interesting because Danceny himself gives so much significance to this act of responding, the simple gesture of writing:

> J'ai reçu vos serments de vivre toujours pour moi. Ah! recevez le mien de consacrer ma vie entière à votre bonheur; recevez-le, et soyez sûr que je ne le trahirai pas. (Letter 31, p. 63)

Despite such an enthusiastic tone, Cécile has only answered his letter, she has not accorded him what the *romanciers libertins* call her "favors." Nonetheless, the connection is clear in Danceny's mind. This letter is but a promise, responding but a first step in a series of interconnected actions that will lead to something as yet unnamed but certainly implied:

> pourquoi ne puis-je sans cesse tenir cette jolie main qui m'a écrit je vous aime! la couvrir de baisers, et me venger ainsi du refus que vous m'avez fait d'une faveur plus grande? (Letter 31, p. 63)

For Danceny as for Valmont, one of the chief implications of being a reader is sexual. The passage just quoted illustrates perfectly the irresistible impulsion that pulls an originally hesitant reader like Cécile or the Présidente de Tourvel deeper and deeper into the readerly and sexual labyrinth. Now that Cécile has replied, she risks the dangers that having answered poses. Encouraged by her act of responding, Danceny is already asking for more obviously sexual concessions: to hold her hand and to cover it with kisses. Danceny and Valmont, the callow youth and the accomplished rake, both assume that responding contains a sexual component. The reader's position therefore does imply a sexual interpretation, especially when the reader is a woman.

The Dangers of Reading

Since the apparently innocent act of receiving letters leads to such catastrophic results as the death of Mme de Tourvel and Cécile's permanent retreat to a convent, it is obvious that reading is a dangerous activity. In addition to the war which eventually breaks out between Valmont and Merteuil and which is waged with weapons they acquired from reading, there are other perils which, although less discussed, nonetheless throw the danger of being a reader into a particularly clear light.

Mme de Volanges knows that Cécile has broken social codes in writing to Danceny and in receiving letters from him. Guilt is more a social than a moral matter for her so she thinks that hiding Cécile's misconduct is a sufficient solution. She considers her daughter's letters troublesome because she is planning her marriage with the Comte de Gercourt, a social advance which might be compromised by this flirtation with Danceny. The mother attempts to repair her daughter's indiscretion by repossessing the potentially dangerous evidence. She demands therefore that Danceny return Cécile's letters:

> Vous trouverez ce-joint le paquet de vos lettres. Je compte que vous me renverrez en échange toutes celles de ma fille. (Letter 62, p. 123)

She hopes to erase any trace of Cécile's misdeed. That word, *trace,* is her own: "et que vous vous prêterez à n['en] laisser aucune trace" (letter 62, p. 123). It is richly significant in our present context, since it echoes Mme de Tourvel who is rightly anxious about the dangerous implications of the letter *as a letter* which she is in the act of writing to the Vicomte:

> j'espère que vous voudrez bien de même me remettre [ma lettre]; je serais vraiment peinée qu'il restât aucune trace d'un événement qui n'eût jamais dû exister. (Letter 26, p. 56)

To trace is perhaps to form a letter with a pen or to write an entire letter. Traces are the remains of any written correspondence, or they may be the after-effects of an unthinking reader's reception of another's tracings or letters. Like Mme de Tourvel, Mme de Volanges fails to recover these traces as she had hoped. First, because Danceny refuses to return Cécile's letters. Second, but more important, because Mme de Volanges focuses on Cécile's fault as a writer and not as a reader. She asks for the letters which her daughter wrote while she returns those she received. Cécile's chief fault, the one which will lead to her own tragic undoing as it does for Mme de Tourvel, is less in writing than in receiving letters. Here the danger is not to write but to read. By returning Danceny's letters, Mme de Volanges compounds her error because in so doing she loses whatever power she might have exercised over him by virtue of possessing his traces. Had she been more perceptive, Mme de Volanges would have understood the danger that threatens her daughter. She is singularly obtuse regarding Cécile, however, and never displays the slightest awareness of who her daughter is and how she should behave as her mother. She does succeed in confiscating Cécile's letters, and thereafter prevents her from writing publicly. Still, Mme de Volanges's focus is on the narrator and the act of writing. She totally ignores the dangerous act of reception.

Despite her mother's vigilance, Cécile remains an active reader. She receives Merteuil's letters, which encourage her to accept Valmont's sexual advances. The latter promises that he will keep her in contact with Danceny and will help her write to him:

> C'est au surplus le seul moyen de continuer à recevoir les lettres de Danceny, et à lui faire passer les vôtres. (Letter 84, p. 187)

Thus she will be able to receive letters from him, which constitutes the third reception in this short sequence! Despite her initial fears, Cécile is seduced through her desire to receive and to read the Chevalier's letters. At first she demurs:

> Malgré tout le plaisir que j'ai, Monsieur, à recevoir les lettres de M. le chevalier Danceny, . . . je n'ai pas osé cependant faire ce que vous me proposez. (Letter 88, p. 201)

Nonetheless she does eventually consent to Valmont's plan and thereby prepares her own tragic fate. The temptation that she cannot resist is the pleasure of reading, the joy of reading Danceny. By misconstruing the real importance of the reader's function as a receiver (listening, accepting, reading), Mme de Volanges in effect delivers her daughter helpless to Merteuil and Valmont.

Anyone who writes to a reader (and who else could or would one write to?) runs a major risk: betrayal. Fear of betrayal motivates the need for confidence that we have already examined. If the writer cannot completely trust his reader, however, he must take other precautions which are then in themselves testimony to the danger that reader represents. The Marquise de Merteuil takes special pains as narrator to avoid the dangers which she so artfully exploits in others as their reader. When writing to Cécile, who is too unformed and guileless to be fully trustworthy, Merteuil gives specific instructions in order to protect herself from any indiscretions, deliberate or otherwise, on the part of her reader:

> car il ne faut pas que vous gardiez cette lettre; et je vous demande et j'exige de vous de la remettre à Valmont aussitôt que vous l'aurez lue. (Letter 105, p. 246)

The Marquise has complete confidence in Valmont, at least for the moment, so she is sure that her letter is safe with him. Still, her fear of other, unwanted readers is so strong that, in the subsequent letter, she repeats this injunction to Valmont. Mme de Merteuil is naturally cautious, a factor which explains why she has been so successful, at least until the novel's denouement, as a female libertine and so generally unsuspected of any such conduct.

While she protects herself from any *faux-pas* on the part of readers like Cécile, the Marquise can seriously imperil her own addressees, who like Mlle de Volanges are less careful than she is. On one occasion her behavior ruthlessly demonstrates how dangerous the simple fact of reading can be. The Marquise brags to Valmont about the pedagogical value of what she has done to Cécile:

> Je crois lui avoir donné une assez bonne leçon sur le danger de garder des lettres, pour oser lui écrire à présent. (Letter 63, p. 129)

Merteuil's lesson consisted in informing Mme de Volanges that her daughter had been carrying on a clandestine correspondence with the Chevalier Danceny. We know the difficulties these dangerous letters posed for both Cécile and Danceny when her mother discovered them: the letters were confiscated, Danceny was banished from the house, and Cécile was frightened out of her wits by her mother's surprise visit to her room. But even this nasty bit of business does not limit the dangerous possibilities inherent in apparently simple letters. Valmont foresees another use these letters could serve, and the danger they could represent for Cécile and even for her mother:

> Mais comme, pour mon compte, j'ai aussi à me venger de la mère, je me réserve en ce cas de déshonorer la fille. Que sait-on? il peut s'engager un procès. Alors, en choisissant bien dans cette correspondance, et n'en produisant qu'une partie, la petite Volanges paraîtrait avoir fait toutes les premières démarches, et s'être absolument jetée à la tête. Quelques-unes des lettres pourraient même compromettre la mère, et *l'entacheraient* au moins d'une négligence impardonnable. (Letter 66, p. 135, italics in original)

The dangers of reading are then legion and subtle. Both Valmont and Merteuil know well how traces can implicate their author and deceive their reader. One phrase in the Marquise's secret account of her seduction and disgracing of Prévan is appropriate here and shows how attentive she is to the danger of having extra readers:

> La soirée ne produisit rien qu'un très petit billet, que le discret amoureux [i.e., Prévan] trouva moyen de me remettre, et que j'ai brûlé suivant ma coutume. (Letter 85, p. 195)

Like Mme de Volanges, the Marquise is greatly concerned by traces (rightly too, given the example of Cécile and Danceny's clandestine correspondence discovered by Mme de Volanges) and therefore she leaves as few as possible. There is perhaps no finer or more convincing tribute to the dangerous potential of the reader than Mme de Merteuil's full awareness of his presence and her constant efforts to escape his notice.

We can point to one last example to show precisely how aware the Marquise is of the danger that a written correspondence represents. Presciently, perhaps tragically, she reminds Valmont of their first encounter, before she began to write to him and therefore before they began to exchange their mutual confidences. She brags that he had no hold over her then because he had no written proof of her intentions or behavior:

> Cependant, si vous eussiez voulu me perdre, quels moyens eussiez-vous trouvés? de vains discours qui ne laissent aucune trace après eux, que votre réputation même eût aidé à rendre suspects, et une suite de faits sans vraisemblance, dont le récit sincère aurait eu l'air d'un roman mal tissu. (Letter 81, p. 180)

Fictional Readers and Their Reading

Again we find that key term *trace*. Words leave no telltale residue behind them; only written letters can constitute unimpeachable proof. As permanent artifacts available to multiple readers and unintended listeners, letters remain as traces that extra readers can read while vain words disappear as soon as they are spoken.

If Mme de Merteuil could completely conceal herself from all readers, there would of course be a gaping hole in the center of this novel. Absolute nondetection is impossible: Merteuil, like the others in the novel, is read. Even though her forethought and her attempts to avoid being read by any reader other than the one she has in mind when writing are eventually frustrated, they are not therefore any less significant. Nor does her failure to avoid the dangers of reading invalidate her recognition of that menace. On the contrary, it only serves to highlight the dangerous threat posed by that fictional reader which even a character as intelligent and as resourceful as the Marquise cannot elude forever.

Writing/Reading: The Ultimate Act

The final characteristic of the fictional reader touches on the quintessential nature of fiction and most especially of the epistolary novel: the two-phased act of writing and reading. To write and to read are the prime, perhaps the only, activities in a letter-novel. What happens outside the ken of these letters is insignificant insofar as it is not reported through them. Writing/reading does not just fashion reality and impose its limits on our perception of that reality. In an epistolary novel, writing can replicate the activity that it is reporting.[6] Whatever words, actions, or types of behavior that Valmont employs to seduce Mme de Tourvel are not real or remain unknown unless they are repeated and/or reported in the letters he writes to her or in those he writes to the Marquise about his courting of the Présidente. That Mme de Tourvel eventually succumbs to the Vicomte's wooing in physical, sexual terms is but the logical extension of what has already happened in terms of writing and, as we have already seen, an inescapable consequence of receiving and responding.

"To read" is implied[7] in the verb *to write* even if in an epistolary novel we do not immediately think of the reader of a letter as quickly as we imagine the writer:

> Cette dépendance confirme la loi sémiologique générale selon laquelle "je" et "tu," l'émetteur et le récepteur d'un énoncé, apparaissent toujours ensemble.[8]

In Todorov's sense, writing and reading are synonymous. Such an interchangeability is further presumed by the seemingly natural sequence of these verbs when we speak of "reading and writing" which does not necessarily indicate the logical sequence of these two actions. Especially in a novel where a personage like Mme de Merteuil warns Cécile about the necessity of knowing precisely to whom and for whom one is writing, there can be no doubt that every narrator writes to a reader who is equally well defined and fully realized.[9] The reciprocal relationship of writer and reader is especially emphasized in this polyphonic epistolary novel. With only two minor exceptions, all the correspondences are two-way exchanges, each character playing in turn both addresser and addressee, emitter and receptor.

To write/read is a basic enabling act since, on a practical level, without writing/reading the novel itself would not exist. However, writing here is not simply language in its purely instrumental function. Rather it goes well beyond this pragmatic mode to become self-referential and even symbolic. It is writing of this latter kind that establishes the complex interconnection of writers and readers within the novel. Without appearing to be different from normal language, writing in the *Liaisons dangereuses* rises to a level that incorporates any plot element easily and effectively while at the same time it can replace the extradiegetic world of events outside the fiction by an entirely self-referential discourse, a text whose own writing becomes the subject of its writing, a writing which contains its own reading.[10] This displacement of plot by discourse is summed up in Cécile's comment to Mme de Merteuil, "comme vous avez bien senti qu'il me serait plus facile de vous écrire que de vous parler" (letter 27, p. 57). Unless writing is set at this high level of extra significance and symbolic import, these exchanges of letters among people who see and speak to each other, often on a daily basis, and who are for a long period isolated together in a single château, would be impossible to justify.[11] Once we recognize that the actual writing and the reading, i.e., the text we have before us, is in fact "all that happened" and accept external facts as dependent on the writing about them and not vice versa, the novel becomes perfectly logical in its own terms, that is, in its self-referential and closed (con)text. Such a valorization of the impact of writing/reading gives more punch to a story of multiple deceptions and of numerous lives destroyed thereby.

Writing/reading then is not just Laclos's choice of a popular novel format which has since been largely abandoned by novelists. On the contrary, Laclos has found a fundamental connection between his story of deception, seduction, and licentious behavior and the narrative technique of telling it through the letters of the participants. Writing is not imposed on a content from outside; rather it springs up internally from the needs and the dynamic of that content as the subject matter seeks its most appropriate form. Like the reader who is always logically present but who is almost always overlooked or ignored, this special characteristic of writing appears to be self-evident. It is important enough to warrant repeating, however. Writing/reading in the *Liaisons dangereuses* contains in and of itself a good portion of the sexual pleasure, the carnal desire, and the delight in deception that constitute the content of this novel.

Cécile Volanges feels a pleasure which is profoundly sexual in nature when she receives her first letter from Danceny. According to the symbolic code of language we have just mentioned, reading functions as the sexual communication or exchange that Cécile is forbidden to enjoy but which she ardently wishes to experience. According to a less rigorous social code, represented by Mme de Volanges, writing is just an indiscretion, a breach of good manners, a lapse in correct behavior, which is liable to misinterpretation and thus able to jeopardize the possibility of an advantageous marriage. Intuitively Cécile feels the emotional and sexual charge that writing/reading contains. She describes what she feels upon receiving Danceny's letter:

> c'est ce jour-là que M. le chevalier Danceny m'a écrit: oh! je vous assure que quand j'ai trouvé sa lettre, je ne savais pas du tout ce que c'était. Mais, pour ne pas mentir, je ne peux pas dire que je n'aie eu bien du plaisir en la lisant. (Letter 27, p. 57)

Despite her "not knowing" what this letter really was and despite her protests "not to lie," Cécile does in fact hide some of the truth. She is very much aware of what this letter represents. In a more candid and revealing letter to her special reader and confidante Sophie, Cécile reveals the powerful sexual impression the letter made upon her. Danceny had hidden it in her harp case, and Cécile will lock it up in a drawer in her secretary later, details that Freudians can ponder at length. She finds it after performing for her mother's friends and then goes to sleep dreaming of the letter and of Danceny:

> et, quand j'ai été couchée, je l'ai tant répétée, que je ne songeais pas à dormir. Dès que je fermais les yeux, je le voyais-là, qui me disait lui-même tout ce que je venais de lire. Je ne me suis endormie que bien tard; et aussitôt que je me suis réveillée (il était encore de bien bonne heure), j'ai été reprendre sa lettre pour la relire à mon aise. Je l'ai emportée dans mon lit, et puis je l'ai baisée, comme si... C'est peut-être mal fait de baiser une lettre comme ça? mais je n'ai pas pu m'en empêcher. (Letter 16, p. 36, ellipsis in original)

That she was projecting her own subconscious desires onto this letter and was naive or innocent enough to remain unaware of what her behavior ("and then I kissed it as if . . .") really meant, is beside the question. What is pertinent is that reading this letter has aroused her sexually just as if Danceny himself were present. For Cécile, reading this letter in her bed translates her obvious desire to receive Danceny there. Reading and receiving, which we have defined as the reader's privileged actions, acquire here their fullest and most potent significance, and one that is totally congruent with the novel's sexual content.

Cécile's initiation to sex and to matters sexual takes place through letters. More accurately we could say that her first sexual experience is a written and a read one. This provocative mixture of the sexual and the textual defines the emotions Cécile feels for the Chevalier. She answers his letter despite her own misgivings and her knowledge that her mother would disapprove. When he finds her response in that same harp case, he is overjoyed. Positioning himself so Mme de Volanges cannot see what he is doing, he squeezes Cécile's hand. To Cécile's written gesture he responds with a touch that is highly sexual:

> ce ne fut qu'un moment: mais je ne saurais te dire le plaisir que cela m'a fait. (Letter 18, p. 40)

Cécile herself connects the pleasure felt in that brief physical contact with Danceny (even if it was mostly imagined) to her role as a reader, receiving, responding, and eventually writing:

> Mais quel mal peut-il y avoir à écrire, surtout quand c'est pour empêcher quelqu'un d'être malheureux? (Letter 18, p. 40)

Her argument is ingenuous, but it nevertheless pinpoints the close ties and even the interchangeability between the physical manifestation of sex and the production of discourse, the act of writing. Writing produces the same effects in Cécile as physical lovemaking would:

> A mesure que le moment de lui écrire approche, mon cœur bat que ça ne se conçoit pas. (Letter 18, p. 40)

This remark echoes the terms Cécile used in the opening letter of the novel to describe the rush of emotion and the physical thrill she felt when she thought (mistakenly, as it turned out) her fiancé had just come to pay her a surprise visit:

> Il vient d'arrêter un carrosse à la porte. . . . Je ne suis pas habillée, la main me tremble et le cœur me bat. (Letter 1, p. 8)

Cécile's symptoms are clearly sexual in nature, whether their cause is the expectation of meeting her future husband or the act of writing her lover.

Danceny can bear further witness to the congruence of writing and sexual activity, although in another context and with another woman. It is the Marquise who, having aroused the Chevalier to fever pitch, receives a letter which posits a continuity between writing and sex:

> En attendant le bonheur de te revoir, je me livre, ma tendre amie, au plaisir de t'écrire. (Letter 150, p. 350)

The familiarity implied in the rarely used *tu*-form and the enthusiastic tone of this letter leave little doubt as to the full sense of *bonheur* and *voir* which are in significant parallel with *plaisir* and *écrire*. The actual joys of sex are not fundamentally different from those of the letter:

> Te retracer mes sentiments, me rappeler les tiens, est pour mon cœur une vraie *jouissance*. (Letter 150, p. 350, my emphasis)

Then as now, *jouissance* meant sexual climax. The choice of the adjective *vraie* is therefore especially meaningful even though Danceny is speaking in hyperbole. This letter's sexual subtext—or perhaps we should say the text's sexual letters—is amplified later:

> Mais une lettre est le portrait de l'âme. Elle n'a pas, comme une froide image, cette stagnance si éloignée de l'amour; elle se prête à tous nos mouvements: tour à tour elle s'anime, elle jouit, elle se repose. (Letter 150, p. 351)

For Danceny, this letter evokes Merteuil in all her physical attractiveness. Those three final verbs imply equally the stages of sexual activity: arousal and foreplay (*animer*); climax (*jouir* echoes its previous use); and post-coital relaxation (*se reposer*). For the Chevalier then, writing letters and making love are not exclusive nor even discrete activities. Rather they are continuous. To the extent that they relay and prolong each other, they are identical:

> je te quitte bien vite, pour t'aller retrouver plus tôt. (Letter 150, p. 352)

When Valmont undertakes the licentious education of Cécile and instructs her in the art of love, he gives to all his lessons a fillip that again equates sex and language:

> J'occupe mon loisir . . . à composer une espèce de catéchisme de débauche, à l'usage de mon écolière. . . . Ce contraste de la candeur naïve avec le langage de l'effronterie ne laisse pas de faire de l'effet. (Letter 110, p. 261)

To be sure, there are blasphemous implications in this passage too. Sacrilege does play a preponderant role in the libertine conduct of both Valmont and Merteuil. Still, it is the close connection of sex and language that interests us the most here. Cécile's progress under Valmont's tutorship is presented as primarily linguistic and it is this unusual aspect of Cécile's debauching that excites Valmont most: "je ne sais pourquoi, il n'y a plus que les choses bizarres qui me plaisent" (letter 110, p. 261). Emphasis falls on how she speaks of sex or how she uses certain words rather than on the physical activity itself. True, even a licentious eighteenth-century novel respected certain norms of decency and *bienséance* in what it would or would not describe. Then too the letter format would logically exclude certain kinds of descriptions since Valmont knows they would not interest the Marquise. She is intent on her revenge against Gercourt and not on the mechanics of Valmont's amorous technique. But it is precisely our contention that Laclos has succeeded in transforming these limitations into strengths. The case for equating writing and sex is very cogent here. Cécile's slide into physical debauchery is foremost an element of discourse. It begins with those letters to and from Danceny and climaxes with Valmont's vocabulary lessons.

The Vicomte highlights the sexual pleasure inherent in writing when, in the early stages of their relationship, he implores Mme de Tourvel to accept his letters. To borrow some of Roland Barthes's terms, perhaps we should speak of these letters as the *plaisir du texte,* since these are the letters that contribute directly to Valmont's eventual *jouissance* with the Présidente. The pertinent question is whether the special pleasure that comes from writing does or does not entirely displace the more conventional joys of sex. Valmont defends his right to write (which is in fact his intention to wrong) the Présidente:

> Pour prix de ce sacrifice, vous m'avez permis de vous écrire, et aujourd'hui vous voulez m'ôter cet unique plaisir. Me le laisserai-je ravir, sans essayer de le défendre? Non, . . . c'est le seul qui me reste, et je le tiens de vous. (Letter 58, p. 118)

That adjective *unique* is richly and appropriately ambivalent. Does it mean that writing to Mme de Tourvel is the only pleasure in his life, that she is in fact his true love? or does it signify that writing is the sole pleasure she has thus far permitted him? Until he possesses her physically and sexually, writing will have to be a substitute, in the Derridian sense of *supplément* and in that sense it is *unique.*

It is this intimate connection between writing/reading and sexuality—we might almost dare to say the interchangeability between these two activities—that permeates Mme de Tourvel's relationship with Valmont. When the latter requests the Père Anselme to arrange a last meeting with the Présidente, the good priest talks of letters while the Vicomte intends sex and seduction. Replying to Valmont, Anselme confirms that "[v]otre lettre sera reçue" (letter 123, p. 288). Similarly, Mme de Tourvel understands that the purpose of this interview touches only on writerly matters:

> je juge que l'objet principal est de me rendre mes lettres qu'il avait gardées jusqu'ici, malgré la demande contraire que je lui avais faite. (Letter 124, p. 289)

Although equally mistaken, the Présidente is nonetheless closer to the truth than Anselme since these letters, their very exchange, and the dispute over returning them have acquired a supplementary sexual significance. Throughout the novel Mme de Tourvel has been trying to refuse receiving and reading Valmont as well as to repossess her own written replies to his advances. After she has surrendered physically to Valmont, Mme de Tourvel sees him with Emilie in his carriage in a traffic jam outside the Opéra. She suspects she has been betrayed. To salvage what is left of her virtue and her self-esteem, she closes her door to the Vicomte and once again asks that those symbolical, sexually charged letters be returned to her:

> Ce billet a donc moins pour objet de vous prier de n'y plus venir [chez elle], que de vous redemander des lettres qui n'auraient jamais dû exister. (Letter 136, pp. 322-23)

Even as she attempts to repossess the traces of her sin and seduction, Mme de Tourvel cannot avoid producing another letter, yet another trace, in her vain efforts to abolish the vicious sexual circle of writing and reading.

Although we have tried to show the close proximity if not the identity of the sexual and the writing activities, writing/reading must be more than that if we are to characterize it as the ultimate act. In addition to its role in procuring sex, therefore, we maintain that writing/reading is also the most powerful weapon in the libertine arsenal for doing harm to others. Since injuring another, like seduction, is active, it is again the narrator who initiates those attacks. The reader, consequently, tends to be the victim in the passive, receptive role as receiver. Writing sets off these complementary pairs and relegates the narrator to the role of attacker and injurer and the reader to that of suffering victim. It is therefore in the real and literal sense that Valmont kills the Présidente when and because he sends her the *Adieu, ce n'est pas ma faute* message. This letter proves to the Présidente that Valmont never loved her. Her reaction to it demonstrates convincingly the deadly power that a letter can wield:

> Le voile est déchiré.... La funeste vérité m'éclaire.... Je vous envoie la lettre que j'ai reçue hier; je n'y joindrai aucune réflexion, elle les porte avec elle. (Letter 143, p. 336)

As it tears away the illusion of Valmont's love, this letter becomes a murderous gesture, it transports a lethal message. Although her actual death is not reported until letter 165, some twenty-two letters later, it is here that the Présidente receives the first wound by letter. A subsequent and equally powerful blow awaits her, as Mme de Volanges reports:

> Un événement, bien indifférent en apparence, mais bien cruel par les suites qu'il a eues, a rendu l'état de la malade au moins aussi fâcheux qu'il était auparavant, si même il n'a pas empiré. (Letter 149, p. 347)

This event is none other than another letter from Valmont which plunges the Présidente further into the troubling darkness of madness from which she will emerge only through death.

> Par malheur, on apporta alors une lettre pour elle. Quand on voulut la lui remettre, elle répondit n'en vouloir recevoir aucune. . . . mais ses propos sans suite nous apprirent seulement que le délire était revenu. (Letter 149, p. 349)

Even more than the actual sexual acts evoked at length in letter 125 but described only sketchily (and some of which might qualify as rape), these two letters deliver the fatal blows that reduce the Présidente to madness and produce her death. These letters are literally acts that kill. They encourage us to accept the concept that letters in this novel are more than written exchanges; they are also action.

Mme de Tourvel begins to die when she receives the cruel *Adieu* message and understands that Valmont has grossly deceived her. Her subsequent and last letter, number 161, is the product of a deranged mind, the directionless utterings of an individual at death's door. As pointed out earlier, this letter has no clearly defined reader or addressee, a fact that Mme de Volanges discovers to her great surprise:

> J'y ai trouvé l'écrit que je vous envoie, qui en effet ne s'adresse à personne pour s'adresser à trop de monde. (Letter 160, p. 367)

Thus it violates the rules of discourse and epistolary exchange that the rest of the novel respects. In a powerful convergence, Mme de Tourvel loses everything: her illusions about Valmont, her love, her mind, her reader, her control over her own words, and her ability to address them coherently to a specific individual. In short she loses her life. She disappears from the novel, and is no longer a viable participant either as writer or as reader. Her own epitaph, as it were, is couched in terms of reading and of the role that she has played as the recipient of Valmont's letters and the butt of his attacks throughout the novel. Now as she dies, and only because she dies, does she escape from the trap of reading and replying:

> ne m'avez-vous pas mise dans l'impossibilité de vous écouter comme de vous répondre? N'attendez plus rien de moi. Adieu, Monsieur. (Letter 161, p. 370)

This time, her decision to cease being a reader is inflexible, even as her previous attempts to stop accepting Valmont's letters never were. This time, her decision is definitive and irrevocable. She will indeed accept no more letters, she will neither listen nor respond; finally she renounces the role of reading which has been a major factor in facilitating her seduction and in thereby leading to her death. Mme de Tourvel's letter without a reader marks an end point in the writer/reader logic that governs the novel; it demonstrates the loss of her sanity and of her life just as her continued exchange of letters with Valmont marked her slow succumbing to his seduction. Words are no longer descriptive;

Fictional Readers and Their Reading

on the contrary, they become active agents which produce the very phenomena they simultaneously record.

It is a written letter that Mme de Merteuil demands from Valmont as proof of his successful seduction of the Présidente. Nothing else will suffice, nothing else can bear the same significance for the Marquise as the handwritten proof of Mme de Tourvel's downfall. Merteuil desires this letter so intensely because it would mark her definitive triumph as a libertine. In a single stroke she would win the proof of the virtuous Présidente's sin and the confirmation of her superiority over Valmont. To write such a letter would be an admission, on the Présidente's part, of her defeat and humiliation at Valmont's hands. But Mme de Tourvel refuses to pen this much-desired letter and dies in silence, heartbroken over her betrayal. We can assume then that she has been beaten but not defeated. Since this is a novel which requires that its characters write to each other (this is after all the basic assumption which justifies the epistolary format), the Présidente's refusal to write becomes a most significant statement. By not writing, Mme de Tourvel again confirms the irresistible power that the written word holds over all the characters in this novel. Not to write denies to both Valmont and Merteuil the proof, which must be read, that their libertine code demands. Not to write thwarts them of their victory; not to write, even as she dies, signifies a belated but nonetheless welcome triumph for the Présidente. Not to write means that she escapes because she cannot be read. With her eloquent but mortal silence the Présidente frustrates both the Vicomte and the Marquise of their expected prey and displays a readerly resistance she never could when she wrote to Valmont.

One final example of the force inherent in writing and its concomitant activity, reading, can be found in Danceny's last letter to Valmont. Danceny has just discovered that Valmont has debauched his beloved Cécile and in so doing has betrayed their confidence and friendship. Inevitably, a duel must follow. The Chevalier has been so ingenuous throughout the novel, and so gullible at Valmont's hands during this entire incident, that only totally unimpeachable evidence will suffice to open his eyes to his own folly. Only writing can provide the irrefutable certainty to convince Danceny that the Vicomte has indeed tricked him:

J'ai vu la preuve de votre trahison écrite de votre main. (Letter 162, p. 370)

The very terms Danceny chooses to express his rage enhance our concept that these letters constitute a closed and self-referential discourse whose prime component is writing these same letters. For Danceny as was the case for Merteuil, proof must be written, the very fact of betrayal can only be established by an act of writing which attains its full term only when it is read. We can then seriously if somewhat paradoxically make the claim that the hand which, indirectly, kills Valmont is the same hand that wrote the incriminating and therefore fatal letter: his own.[12]

With Valmont's death, the double act of writing/reading closes back upon itself. Early in the novel Merteuil warned Valmont of the dangerous, albeit unforeseeable, implications of reading and writing when she denigrated his strategy for seducing the Présidente.

> Mais la véritable école [sottise] est de vous être laissé aller à écrire. Je vous défie de prévoir à présent où ceci peut vous mener. (Letter 33, p. 67)

Writing/reading is a double-edged sword as is the narrative process itself. Just as the narrator is symmetrically doubled by the reader to whom he writes and on whom he depends for his own actualization, so too does a double, contradictory movement characterize the theory of the fictional reader that we are elaborating here. The confidence that each writer seeks in his reader can be betrayed by that same reader. Receiving letters is active as well as passive. As such, it signals a willingness to engage in a most dangerous form of communication while it places responsibility for that exchange squarely on the reader's shoulders. More than mere reaction, responding is a most critical action that provokes the next move in the war between the sexes. The menace latent in these dangerous connections is equally double since it can strike either the writer or the reader. Writing is itself double since it includes reading as an essential component. Finally, as we shall see in the next chapter, the attempt to write to one specific reader can be complicated and even thwarted by the presence of extra and unknown readers. In an epistolary novel like the *Liaisons dangereuses* composed of such complex exchanges and interceptions, writing/reading is the ultimate act.

3

Hidden Readers

The traditional interpretation of the *Liaisons dangereuses* holds that Valmont is the principal character who maintains simultaneously two critical liaisons and correspondences. The first is his deceptive seduction of Mme de Tourvel, while the second is his rakish and libertine commentary on the first with Mme de Merteuil. As narrator, Valmont is indeed the dominating figure in this novel because he writes more letters than any other personage. Of the one hundred seventy-five letters that comprise the novel, he is the author of fifty-one of them. In comparison, Mme de Merteuil writes only twenty-seven letters while Mme de Tourvel and Cécile account for twenty-four and twenty-five respectively. However, when we adopt the perspective of the addressee, these distributions change and so do their indications of relative strength, influence, and importance within the novel.

Mme de Merteuil, we are not surprised to learn, is the most significant reader in the novel, directly receiving forty-two letters against Valmont's total of thirty-nine. Relative proportions are more impressive here than absolute numbers: Merteuil writes twenty-seven letters but receives forty-two, thus almost doubling her importance as she passes from writer to reader. In Valmont's case, there is a sharp decrease in his narrative importance: he writes fifty-one letters but receives only thirty-nine. Cécile reads only thirteen letters, the Présidente de Tourvel twenty.

These figures concern only the apparent readers, that is the individuals to whom a letter is addressed and sent. I call them "apparent" because they are the obvious, declared, and clearly visible recipients of these missives. Another type of reader does exist, however, who is not apparent and obvious, but who, on the contrary, is secret and hidden. This second type is by far the more interesting. Readers of this type are hidden because they are not the named addressees of the letters they are reading. Secret, invisible, and unrecognized, these readers stand in sharp contrast to those of the first type, who are both known and highly visible. In addition, readers of the second type cannot be wholly identified with the receptors or addressees in Jakobson's communication model (i.e., addresser/emitter—message—addressee/receptor). Rather, they escape from the traditional understanding of the reader/receiver/receptor inside the narrative circuit because they are supplementary, additional readers who pervert the narrative exchange by their very presence and especially by their unauthorized reading activity.

This remote and supplementary reader can be hidden with respect either to the narrator, who does not know who is reading the letters he or she has written; or to the first reader, the legitimate addressee who is unknowingly displaced by this second reading. An apparent reader can be doubled and most often contradicted by such a second reader who reinterprets the letter in question. Whether they are hidden from the narrator or from the intended reader, these secret readers provide additional interpretations for the same facts. They open up new possibilities, they establish new connections that would be impossible were they not there to (re)read.

By creating this second layer of readers, Laclos has enormously enriched his novel. The subject of the *Liaisons dangereuses* is seduction and deception. This narrative material is given an appropriate narrative form through the deceptive activity of the secret readers who owe their very existence to false appearances, duplicity, and unlawful intrusion into the private space of others. The subject described, deceiving others, becomes an integral part of the novel's structure; the manner of the telling fits perfectly the matter of its presentation. Having this extra, secret, and obviously illegal and illegitimate reader on certain critical occasions produces a double layering, a double vision, like sets of mirrors[1] which replicate reality even as they falsify it. In terms simply of letters and written words, which are after all the very stuff of an epistolary novel, what is said is said. It remains clearly and unchangeably printed upon the page. Yet, what those written signals mean and how they are understood depend upon who reads them. Frequently then, an apparently obvious meaning reached by the intended addressee can be transformed into something radically different by the presence of a hidden reader and his (re)reading. To better understand the textual strategies and the sexual struggles among this novel's personages, whom we most often consider narrators and writers of letters, we should begin to view them as readers who are more significant when they receive and read letters.[2]

The hidden reader whose existence I have been trying to establish becomes a more persuasive idea when we turn from theory to an actual illustration of this reading activity at work. The Marquise de Merteuil and the Vicomte de Valmont, the two major figures in this novel, offer us two fine and yet very different examples of the hidden reader in operation. Because each one attains his or her status by a different process, our discussion of these clandestine and illegal acts of reading will also allow us to analyze two differing portraits of seducers and two different methods of seduction. How one becomes a secret reader, who is, let us remember, an unauthorized and perverting force in structural terms, is an especially important question in this novel of duplicity and deception. One interesting conclusion that we will draw from our discussion is an enhanced awareness of the power and importance of the Marquise. Too often she has been considered a mere echo of Valmont, a secondary female rake, a shadow of that prime male seducer. Seen from the perspective of the reader, however, she acquires a much more impressive stature. In fact, she can even be seen as Valmont's superior in all libertine activities and, most pertinently, in the area of reading letters. The Marquise is without a doubt the most powerful and intelligent reader in the novel. The more we understand the reader's role in the functioning of the novel as both a text and a record of seduction, the more we appreciate the Marquise's achievement.

That Laclos himself intended the hidden reader to be such a critical and privileged perspective in his novel, there can be little doubt. In letter 47, which Valmont writes to the Marquise, he also includes another letter.[3] This other letter, 48, is written to Mme de Tourvel, who is therefore the obvious addressee, the apparent reader. But Valmont intends that the Marquise should also read the Présidente's letter. Merteuil therefore becomes the secret reader who reads without the first reader, Mme de Tourvel, knowing that she is present, as a third party, in this exchange which should have only Valmont and Tourvel as emitter and receptor respectively. The postal complication involved here (Valmont asks Merteuil to mail the letter for Tourvel from Paris) is not at all useless. On the contrary, it is necessary. It provides a convenient excuse for Valmont to involve Merteuil as a secret reader without immediately revealing the danger the Vicomte is running. The consequences of secret reading will become apparent later; at present, Valmont seems to be master of this deceptive, double game, amusing the Marquise on one hand and toying with the Présidente on the other. Clearly, the Vicomte is writing a most ironic and cruel letter to the Présidente. While protesting his sincere love for her, he is in fact mocking her, both in what he is saying and in what he is doing. His words are all double-edged, meaning both what they appear to say and something else; in addition, he underscores his disdain for the Présidente by making love to another woman as he writes and as he describes what he is actually doing in an ambiguous and deceitful manner. It is the presence of two different readers that makes Valmont's ploy successful. Mme de Tourvel understands only the surface of the letter, its superficial meaning, while the Marquise enjoys a deeper comprehension of all that is going on. Valmont compliments Merteuil by allowing her so intimate a view of his private correspondence and thereby indicates her superiority over the Présidente in his own eyes. Thus Valmont attempts to convince Merteuil that he prefers her to the Présidente. Both Valmont's words and deeds illustrate his narrative and rakish skills. In terms of sex, he enjoys Emilie while mocking Mme de Tourvel;

in terms of readers, he speaks through the Présidente to the Marquise by using an elliptical code that only the latter understands.

As readers of the entire novel and more precisely of this sequence of two letters, we realize the interplay of the two readers and the value of that second reading, Merteuil's, which completes the full meaning of letter 48. Read alone and out of its crucial context this letter might be construed to mean only what it seems to say. In context, however, it accumulates supplementary meanings which are latent in the text but which remain invisible at first reading and especially for the addressee or the apparent recipient. As readers of the entire novel, we are not fooled like Mme de Tourvel because we notice that Laclos has rearranged the natural, chronological presentation of these two letters. Letter 48 is written first and then Valmont writes the sequel, 47, to the Marquise. This temporal disruption draws our attention and demands an effort to find an explanation and a deeper meaning beneath this surface. By inverting the order of these letters, Laclos assures that we shall learn the perverted sense, the second reading, the hidden addressee's interpretation before seeing the first one, the incorrect understanding, the apparent recipient's mistaken comprehension of it. The gap between the two significations of this one single letter thereby becomes unmistakable. The presence of the additional reader is made most evident by the modified, nonchronological sequence of these letters, and it affects their meaning. Such a disturbed chronology is but one formal manner of indicating that a second reader is at work, changing a message's meaning and perverting the truth. It also demonstrates that the first or most complete reading of any text is in fact the second. The ultimate significance of any letter cannot be established by a single reading, nor by a single reader, nor at a single moment in time. Despite the fixed nature of the text, as words written or printed on a page, unchanged and unchanging, its meaning can be fluid and elusive, dependent upon the multiple contexts in which the text is read and upon the multiple readers who fashion and refashion its implications according to their own thinking . . . or rather reading.

Let us now examine in some detail the two principal characters whose presence as hidden readers in the text gives them a tremendous advantage in all their libertine projects. Each one becomes a secret reader in a different manner which seems to correspond closely to his or her personality. Valmont himself notices the distinction between his own libertine style and Merteuil's seductive strategies:

> Tandis que, maniant avec adresse les armes de votre sexe, vous triomphiez par la finesse; moi, rendant à l'homme ses droits imprescriptibles, je subjuguais par l'autorité. (Letter 96, p. 215)

While these differences are in no sense absolute, they are valid enough to distinguish between the two and to formulate a typology of the secret reader.

Merteuil, as a woman, relies on her intuitive subtlety, while Valmont, the male, imposes by brute force and strength.

Valmont: The Reader as Thief

We turn first to the Vicomte de Valmont, the perfect rake, who undertakes to seduce the Présidente de Tourvel and to debauch Cécile Volanges. To carry off this double seduction successfully, Valmont becomes a secret, hidden reader in a manner that tells a great deal about his own character as well as about the type of power he acquires as spy or eavesdropper on other correspondents.

The method most characteristic of Valmont is to steal the letters he wants. Such an intrusion into the communication model and the narrative exchange is obviously a violent and illegal one. It is appropriate to the impetuous and aggressive masculine qualities of Valmont, but it at the same time betrays a lack of sophistication on his part. The Marquise de Merteuil often chides the Vicomte because he lacks, in her estimation, the intelligence and skill needed to become a secret reader in any more demanding manner:

> Ah! mon pauvre Valmont, quelle distance il y a encore de vous à moi! Non, tout l'orgueil de votre sexe ne suffirait pas pour remplir l'intervalle qui nous sépare. Parce que vous ne pourriez exécuter mes projets, vous les jugez impossibles! Etre orgueilleux et faible, il te sied bien de vouloir calculer mes moyens et juger de mes ressources! Au vrai, Vicomte, vos conseils m'ont donné de l'humeur, et je ne puis vous le cacher. (Letter 81, p. 172)

Stealing letters is not the Marquise's method. Whatever lack of cunning or expertise Valmont's violence betrays, however, it does make him a hidden reader. What interests us here are the results of Valmont's larceny and the advantages that he gains as a thief.

In letter 44, Valmont recounts to the Marquise how he succeeded in stealing certain letters written to and received by Mme de Tourvel. Not accidentally, the stage for this crime is set when Valmont's valet undertakes the seduction of the Présidente's chamber servant. This provides an amusing echo in the supporting cast of the main action played by the principals. Here Laclos cleverly exploits the technique of double plots juxtaposing masters and valets which was so common in eighteenth-century theater.[4] In the middle of the night, Valmont interrupts these lovers, sends his valet away, and playing the incongruous role of honest judge and custodian of morals, he browbeats and intimidates the girl into betraying her mistress:

> Comme je sentis que plus cette fille serait humiliée, plus j'en disposerais facilement, je ne lui permis de changer ni de situation [she is in bed] ni de parure [and

> naked]; ... je m'assis à côté d'elle sur le lit qui était fort en désordre, et je commençai ma conversation. Comme j'avais besoin de garder l'empire que la circonstance me donnait sur elle, je conservai un sang-froid qui eût fait honneur à la continence de Scipion. (Letter 44, p. 92)

Valmont drives a hard bargain. The price of his silence will be the girl's turning over to him "les poches de sa maîtresse," which means all the letters that Mme de Tourvel has received while at the château. Valmont is careful not to disturb the order of these letters since he will return them so that the Présidente will never suspect he has seen them.

> Une fois maître de ce trésor, je procédai à l'inventaire avec la prudence que vous me connaissez: car il était important de remettre tout en place. (Letter 44, p. 93)

What he really wants, and what this detail of replacing emphasizes, is a matter of contents. Valmont wants to read these letters in secret, over the shoulder of the Présidente as it were, and seize their message. Such a secret reading will give him a critical advantage over her. Knowing the other's secret, and especially knowing it secretly, comprises an essential part of Valmont's campaign of seduction against Mme de Tourvel:

> je masquai l'impatience où j'étais de voir arriver l'heure qui devait me livrer le secret qu'on s'obstinait à me cacher. (Letter 44, p. 93)

Were the Présidente capable of protecting her text from Valmont's larceny, she would be better able to protect herself from his sexual advances. Seducing the Présidente is done by and through letters, literally; her seduction is verbal in the fullest sense of the word. For us, reading the entire novel, we can appreciate to what point this seduction is in the letters themselves as letters. Thus, when Valmont steals the Présidente's letters, enjoys them, and possesses them physically, even if only temporarily, we can see these actions as being sexually symbolic. All these verbs, *steal, enjoy,* and *possess,* enhance the main theme of sexual seduction and at the same time enlarge the illegal and immoral ramifications of Valmont's conduct. In French, Valmont *détourne* (turns away from an original goal) these letters literally just as he *détourne* (debauches) Mme de Tourvel morally.

But what does Valmont actually learn from reading the Présidente's letters? What precisely is the advantage or the power he acquires as a secret reader? First, he gains a brief glimpse into the Présidente's domestic life which he naturally deprecates:

> Je tombai d'abord sur deux lettres du mari, mélange indigeste de détails de procès et de tirades d'amour conjugal, que j'eus la patience de lire en entier, et où je ne trouvai pas un mot qui eût rapport à moi. (Letter 44, pp. 93-94)

The stolid and respectable Président no doubt offers a sharp contrast to the dashing and gallant Valmont, both stylistically in his letters (the Vicomte naturally finds them boring), and by extension, socially and personally. Behind the novel's sexual struggles lies another battle, a social conflict that pits the declining *noblesse d'épée,* personified by Valmont here, against the *noblesse de robe,* magistrates like the Président, and their natural allies, the rising bourgeoisie.[5] The Marquise at one point clearly intends to insult the Présidente by referring to her as a *bourgeoise.* The social reality, the class struggle, and the snobism of the *ancien régime* find an echo in the background of this novel about seduction and sexual conquests. Such referentiality is indirect, however. This epistolary novel is decidedly self-contained: its constituent letters are its prime reality. They are both the vehicles for the content as well as that content itself. We have already stated that writing is a form of seduction, a way for libertine to attack victim; now we are seeing that reading can be an equally effective strategy in a rogue's libertine behavior.

Next, Valmont finds letters from Mme de Volanges and immediately recognizes that it is she who has been warning the Présidente against him. This is a great strategic victory, since now he knows whose credit to diminish, whose opinions to refute, in order to negate the impact of these warnings.

> Qui croyez-vous qui veuille me perdre auprès de cette femme que j'adore? quelle furie supposez-vous assez méchante, pour tramer une pareille noirceur? (Letter 44, p. 94)

Valmont's anger is unjustified since Mme de Volanges is only telling the truth about him. But it is also explicable because he never suspected her of this disservice. Knowledge is indeed power. Furthermore, this bit of information will lead to a terrible retribution, since it provokes Valmont's cooperation with the Marquise in debauching Cécile, Mme de Volanges's daughter. A complete rake, Valmont does not hesitate to pervert even sex into a method for debasing another and for securing vengeance for himself:

> Ah! sans doute il faut séduire sa fille: mais ce n'est pas assez, il faut la perdre; et puisque l'âge de cette maudite femme la met à l'abri de mes coups, il faut la frapper dans l'objet de ses affections. (Letter 44, p. 94)

Still the most desired information concerns Mme de Tourvel herself and her reactions to the advances Valmont has been making. Up to this point, Valmont has been guessing about her. Sometimes he appears to win her confidence, at other times he loses it. Doubts bedevil the Vicomte as he tries to ascertain, for example, the full effect of his benevolent action upon Mme de Tourvel. His benevolence was an act of real generosity: Valmont did after all pay the debts of a poor family that was on the point of being evicted from its home. However, it was also false in that Valmont had arranged the spontaneous action and stage-managed the whole scene. His purpose was to impress the Présidente. Despite his apparent success, he could not know for sure what she was thinking about him and how she was reacting to this new information about his noble nature. Consequently, he was reduced to making deductions based on appearances, as his choice of verbs clearly indicates:

> Des regards, plus doux encore que de coutume, et presque caressants, me firent bientôt deviner. . . . Pendant ce temps, j'observais . . . ce son de voix qui, par son altération déjà sensible, trahissait l'émotion de son cœur. . . . mais moi, je m'aperçus bien que sa main tremblante ne lui permettait pas de continuer son ouvrage. (Letter 23, pp. 48-49)

As fine and as carefully noted as these observations are, they can only be subjective interpretations, as much imagined as seen, and therefore all liable to error. Desperately Valmont needs to know without any shadow of a doubt the Présidente's true reactions. Now, thanks to this theft of her letters, he will learn the truth and this directly from the Présidente herself. As a secret reader assisted by this supplementary reading of her letters, he will be able to spy upon Mme de Tourvel's secret thoughts and to ascertain her true feelings for him.

Before continuing our analysis of Valmont's theft, we should clarify the confusing series of letters and events which leads up to it. At the beginning of her acquaintanceship with Valmont, Mme de Tourvel refused to accept his letters. In order to make her his reader, the Vicomte has to resort to a number of subterfuges, which he in due course recounts to the Marquise. The delivery and reception of his first letter take place under rather amusing circumstances. While the Présidente is ill in bed, the Vicomte and Mme de Rosemonde pay her a visit:

> Je saisis un moment, où Mme de Rosemonde s'était éloignée, pour remettre ma lettre: on refusa de la prendre; mais je la laissai sur le lit, et allai bien honnêtement approcher le fauteuil de ma vieille tante, qui voulait être auprès *de son cher enfant*: il fallut bien serrer la lettre pour éviter le scandale. (Letter 25, pp. 53-54, italics in original)

Thus Valmont invents the first in a series of ruses which he must employ each time he wants to write the Présidente at this initial stage of their relationship. Valmont can never be certain that he will succeed and he constantly fears that Mme de Tourvel will avoid receiving and reading his letters. In a later letter to the Marquise, Valmont reports the various ruses he has used and the little battle of wits that each one entails:

> Depuis l'affaire du 19 [i.e., the incident quoted above], mon inhumaine, qui se tient sur la défensive, a mis à éviter les rencontres une adresse qui a déconcerté

la mienne. . . . Mes lettre mêmes sont le sujet d'une petite guerre: non contente de n'y pas répondre, elle refuse de les recevoir. Il faut pour chacune une ruse nouvelle, et qui ne réussit pas toujours.

Vous vous rappelez par quel moyen simple j'avais remis la première [letter 24, the incident quoted above]; la seconde [letter 35] n'offrit pas plus de difficulté. Elle m'avait demandé de lui rendre sa lettre [number 26, her reaction to letter 24]: je lui donnai la mienne en place, sans qu'elle eût le moindre soupçon. Mais soit dépit d'avoir été attrapée, soit caprice, ou enfin soit vertu, car elle me forcera d'y croire, elle refusa obstinément la troisième [letter 36]. (Letter 34, p. 69)

Valmont's efforts to make the Présidente his reader recall a crucial component of the reader's make-up which we have already examined. To receive a letter is to open the narrative exchange, to permit the circuit to function, and, thus, to become responsible for the consequences of that communication. To accept a letter signifies the willingness to become a reader with all that being a reader implies. Mme de Tourvel's attempts to reject Valmont and not to read his letters show that she is at least dimly aware of the perils of becoming his reader and that at this stage in their relationship she does try, albeit without success, to avoid those dangers.

Moreover, a chronological discrepancy at this same point signals the importance of reading. In letter 34, which he writes to the Marquise, Valmont describes the Présidente's reception of letter 36. He includes in this letter draft copies of two "previous" letters, numbers 35 and 36. The order in which these letters were written is not identical to the order in which they are read. This disruption of the normal sequence highlights the distance between reading and writing as well as the gap between any innocent reading and a more informed one. Letters should be read several times, in differing sequences, in order to catch their changing significances which depend on the context of the reading itself. Although he wrote these very letters, Valmont himself does not know all that they contain because they have acquired additional meanings since he wrote them, meanings which were added precisely by Mme de Tourvel's act of reading.

Since Valmont was the writer of the very same letters for which he is about to become the secret reader, we should realize what a special situation this is and how significant it is for our discussion of the value of reading and readers in this novel. Valmont's secret reading is a search for the traces, for the smallest indications of the previous reading. Not only is meaning fluid in these letters, but the almost imperceptible fact of having been read can constitute part of a letter's final significance. As spy and secret reader in quest of the minute traces of Mme de Tourvel's own reading, Valmont finds indications which reveal the feelings she is trying to hide from him. He contemplates then

les morceaux de ma fameuse lettre de *Dijon,* soigneusement rassemblés. . . . Jugez de ma joie, en y apercevant les traces, bien distinctes, des larmes de mon adorable dévote. (Letter 44, p. 94)

Once the writer of this letter, Valmont is now its second reader attempting to learn from it something about Mme de Tourvel, its first reader, that he did not know when he wrote it. Just as the growing complexity of the shifting relationships between narrator and reader turns the reading process back upon itself, so too does the entire novel turn and return upon itself, self-referentially, reusing the same material, changing meanings by changing contexts and revising previous letters by subsequent ones.

What Valmont calls the "fameuse lettre de *Dijon*" is letter 36. He falsified the Dijon postmark so that Mme de Tourvel would mistake it as coming from Bourgogne where her husband was tending to his legal duties. Since the Présidente is still refusing to accept any letters from him, this Dijon postmark is yet another of the ruses he imagines to insure the safe delivery of his written advances. To complete the illusion, he disguises his handwriting and slips his letter among those which arrive each day at the château and which are distributed at lunch when everyone is together at table. Mme de Tourvel quickly and eagerly opens this letter but immediately understands what it is and who wrote it:

> le premier coup d'œil l'instruisit; et il se fit une telle révolution sur sa figure, que Mme de Rosemonde s'en aperçut, et lui dit: "Qu'avez-vous?" (Letter 34, p. 71)

The Présidente is angry, embarrassed that Valmont has once again written to her despite her injunction forbidding it, and upset that she has been fooled into receiving and reading his letter.

> La timide dévote n'osait lever les yeux, ne disait mot, et, pour sauver son embarras, feignait de parcourir l'épître, qu'elle n'était guère en état de lire. Je jouissais de son trouble. (Letter 34, p. 71)

Unfortunately for Valmont, he cannot know the secret thoughts and emotions the Présidente is experiencing. He observes carefully, but he cannot be sure that he is interpreting the signs correctly. In any case, Mme de Tourvel's final gesture speaks for itself:

> "Mais la lettre et son auteur m'inspirent un égal mépris. On m'obligera de ne m'en plus parler." En disant ces mots, elle déchira l'audacieuse missive, en mit les morceaux dans sa poche, se leva et sortit. (Letter 34, p. 71)

Judging from these words and actions, one would say that the Présidente has decisively rejected Valmont's new advance. He believes so and consoles himself with a minor technical victory: "Malgré cette colère, elle n'en a pas moins eu ma lettre" (letter 34, p. 71).

Now, thanks to the letters whose contents he has stolen, he learns as a secret reader that the Présidente has repented of her action, reconstituted the torn letter, read it, and wept over it. Valmont's hidden reading produces sweet rapture, a pleasure which is transparently sexual in nature and intensity:

> Je l'avoue, je cédai à un mouvement de jeune homme, et baisai cette lettre avec un transport dont je ne me croyais plus susceptible. (Letter 44, p. 94)

Valmont kissing the Présidente's letter recalls Cécile's going to bed with Danceny's letter.

The tears Mme de Tourvel has shed while reading Valmont's letter and the intimate emotions they betray are not the only traces that the Présidente has left as a reader. As Valmont secretly (re)reads his own letters to her, he is trying to read her reading of him, he is treating these letters like a delicate palimpsest. The passage of each reader remains imprinted on the text for subsequent readers to decipher. Valmont is most pleased with his reading since through it and in it he discovers the proof he wants so badly that the Présidente in fact loves him:

> Je continuai l'heureux examen; je retrouvai toutes mes lettres de suite, et par ordre de dates; et ce qui me surprit plus agréablement encore, fut de trouver la première de toutes, celle que je croyais m'avoir été rendue par une ingrate, fidèlement copiée de sa main; et d'une écriture altérée et tremblante, qui témoignait assez de la douce agitation de son cœur pendant cette occupation. (Letter 44, p. 94)

All these details speak pertinently to our contention that the reader is a crucial presence in this novel. Twice the Présidente affirms her function as reader in spectacular fashion. First, she pieces together the Dijon letter which she had torn to shreds, and thereby negates her original refusal to accept and to read it. Second, by copying in her own hand Valmont's letter (number 24), she in fact keeps that letter even though she ostensibly rejected it and returned it to him in letter 26. By not keeping letter 24, she at first declined to be Valmont's reader, she refused to be the narrator's willing counterpart whose reception of the text permits the communication circuit to function. Now the Vicomte's theft reveals that she has undone her own attempts to reject his epistolary and sexual advances, even though her efforts were so effective. By copying one letter and piecing together the other, she clearly accepts her role as addressee and consequently as partner to the narrator. As reader, she gives sense to Valmont's writing which, without her, would have no object. Without her as receiver and reader, his letters and his plans for seduction would miss their target. Both the Présidente's trembling hand and her copious tears mark her reading of his letters, her acquiescence in her role as his addressee, and her acceptance of his right to speak to her which is synonymous with his right to seduce her. More important for Valmont, they testify to her sincere affection, no matter how hesitant, and even her nascent love for him.

This theft is not the only instance of Valmont's criminal activity. Valmont becomes a thief a second time when, after Mme de Tourvel's flight to Paris, he instructs Azolan to intercept her letters and to forward them to him.

> Il faut que vous m'instruisiez de tout ce qui se passe chez Mme de Tourvel. . . . Songez aussi à vous rendre l'ami de celui qui porte ses lettres à la poste. Offrez-vous souvent à lui pour faire cette commission à sa place; et quand il acceptera, ne faites partir que celles qui vous paraîtront indifférentes, et envoyez-moi les autres, surtout celles à Mme de Volanges, si vous en rencontrez. (Letter 101, p. 233)

In this manner the Vicomte continues to spy on Mme de Tourvel's letters and maintains his position as a hidden reader. He deduces, at one point, "que la légère personne a changé de confidente" (letter 110, p. 258). Again this is but a guess on his part. His suspicion will be confirmed, however, by his illegal tampering with the mails:

> Le seul moyen de me mettre au fait, est, comme vous voyez, d'intercepter le commerce clandestin. J'en ai déjà envoyé l'ordre à mon chasseur; et j'en attends l'exécution de jour en jour. (Letter 110, p. 258)

Even though Azolan does make some comic mistakes about which letters should be intercepted (for example, he reports in letter 107 that he is sending along a letter for the Présidente's husband but that he let one for Mme de Rosemonde pass), Valmont's thievery again produces important results:

> depuis huit jours je suis dans la confidence de ma belle; elle ne me dit pas ses secrets, mais je les surprends. Deux lettres d'elle à Mme de Rosemonde m'ont suffisamment instruit, et je ne lirai plus les autres que par curiosité. (Letter 115, pp. 272-73)

By larceny Valmont acquires a privilege that Mme de Tourvel would surely deny she ever accorded him: he is now in her confidence, not just indirectly but also illegally.

While this second instance of stealing letters is much less dramatic than the first, both combine to reinforce the fact that Valmont becomes a hidden reader unlawfully. He is able to read Mme de Tourvel's letters only because he is a thief. His status as a hidden reader was made possible by seducing and blackmailing the Présidente's maid into stealing her mistress's letters and then by Azolan's interception of other missives. Both these acts are tainted with illegality and immorality. At the same time they are manifestations of strength and violence, of what Valmont called his *autorité*. The Vicomte holds the upper hand and he uses this advantage mercilessly against his social and intellectual inferiors. Not surprisingly, the knowledge he gains from being a secret reader produces equally unscrupulous and immoral behavior. By reading her letters covertly, Valmont has violated Mme de Tourvel's privacy and penetrated her intimate secrets. At this point her observable behavior still conceals the subconscious truth that she refuses to admit even to herself: she loves Valmont. In reading these stolen letters, the Vicomte discovers this truth through the evidence of the Présidente's own reading. His secret reading allows him to observe what is ordinarily invisible and unobservable. What the Présidente is struggling to repress consciously, her own act of reading has revealed inadvertently. Once Valmont knows her weakness and her love for him, he can better plan how to attack her. Without this crucial personal information, which he could never have discovered except as a secret reader, the Vicomte would probably have failed to seduce Mme de Tourvel. At the very least, his courtship/attack would have been much prolonged and she would have resisted him much more successfully. His ultimate success as a libertine and a rake is therefore closely tied to these violent, unlawful actions and to their literary counterpart, his status as a hidden reader. With these two larcenies Valmont violates the social and legal codes that protect the privacy of written correspondence while he also breaks the moral codes that establish the sanctity of marriage, respect among friends, and the personal bonds of love and affection. In so doing, he also exploits the literary code which presumes the existence and the importance of a reader.

One minor character provides another example of a violent, unauthorized, and illegal reading which we can discuss fruitfully in conjunction with Valmont. Like the Vicomte, Mme de Volanges becomes the second reader of a correspondence that was not intended for her. Using her maternal authority, she forces herself into this role as the extra reader of the letters written by Danceny and Cécile to each other. Again like Valmont, she does not owe this situation as an extra and supplementary reader to her own perspicacity or intelligence. On the contrary, she is informed about the existence of these letters and then simply uses her authority as a mother to appropriate her daughter's letters. In contrast to the Vicomte, however, she is not hidden from those she is spying upon. Hence, she is not a secret reader although she is a remote and secondary one. She was not the original addressee but she is the final reader, reading behind the immediate addressees, either Danceny or Cécile, and understanding some implications that escape the correspondents themselves. Since she is not nearly as clever or as cunning as the Vicomte, the power she derives from being an extra reader is not as effective as his. Nonetheless, she does acquire some power simply because she occupies the reader's powerful position. She does, after all, break up Cécile and Danceny even though the unfortunate result of this is that they fall into the clutches of Valmont and Merteuil. Despite her inferiority as a supplementary reader, Mme de Volanges's case is worth investigating because it provides another example of a reader's power which is obtained by illegal and definitely unsubtle means. In addition, since it differs from Valmont's use of violence, it offers proof of the complex layering, echoing, and differentiating that Laclos has achieved in the structure of his novel.

To become an extra reader of her daughter's love letters, Mme de Volanges uses force and surprise, as did Valmont. She enters Cécile's room as the latter is preparing for bed, dismisses the servant and

> me demanda la clef de mon secrétaire, et le ton dont elle me fit cette demande me causa un tremblement si fort, que je pouvais à peine me soutenir. . . . mais enfin il fallut bien obéir. Le premier tiroir qu'elle ouvrit fut justement celui où étaient les lettres du chevalier Danceny. . . . je la vis commencer à lire. . . . Elle a emporté toutes les lettres de Danceny. (Letter 61, pp. 121-22)

Cécile's physical reactions indicate the extent of her mother's violence. She trembles like a leaf throughout the scene and nearly faints:

> J'étais si troublée . . . je me trouvai mal au point que je perdis connaissance. (Letter 61, pp. 121-22)

Once apprised of Cécile's love for Danceny, Mme de Volanges opposes it with all her might. She demands that all contact between the two be broken off immediately and definitively. She accuses Danceny of abusing her confidence as well as Cécile's. In no uncertain terms she informs him that henceforth he is unwelcome in their home and that their door is closed to him (letter 62). More important to Mme de Volanges, it would seem, than the actual courtship are the letters that constitute the exchange between Cécile and Danceny. She demands that the latter return these letters because she fears the consequences should they be read by anyone else. In this Mme de Volanges shows an intelligent respect for unintended readers whose very existence bristles with power and unforeseen ramifications. Unwanted readers and their unwanted readings could destroy Cécile's reputation and thereby ruin the projected marriage to Gercourt. Mme de Volanges is understandably anxious to prevent any such eventuality:

> Je compte que vous me renverrez en échange toutes [les lettres] de ma fille; et que vous vous prêterez à ne laisser aucune trace d'un événement dont nous ne pourrions garder le souvenir, moi sans indignation, elle sans honte, et vous sans remords. (Letter 62, p. 123)

Mme de Volanges is aware enough to recognize that letters leave traces, such as those that Valmont found when he became the Présidente's secret reader, and that such traces can be interpreted to one's disadvantage. Nonetheless Mme de Volanges is ultimately an ineffective reader because she does not know the full value of her position as an intrusion into the private space of others and thus fails to exploit it thoroughly. In the sentence preceding the citation above, she makes the capital mistake of returning Danceny's letters to him: "Vous trouverez ci-joint le paquet de vos lettres" (letter 62, p. 123). This explains the meaning of *en échange*. Danceny, on the other hand, is more perceptive than Mme de Volanges about the value of the reader. While she is willing to give up the traces she possesses, he is not. Although he remains polite and dignified, he is adamant in his refusal to surrender these letters:

> Les lettres de Mlle de Volanges, toujours si précieuses pour moi, me le deviennent bien plus dans ce moment. Elles sont l'unique bien qui me reste; elles seules me retracent encore un sentiment qui fait tout le charme de ma vie. (Letter 64, p. 131)

In a sense Danceny is learning the ropes about the power of the reader, a lesson he will put to good use at the end of the novel after his duel with Valmont and after acquiring reading power over the Marquise de Merteuil. He can see that the reader's advantage comes either from discovering another's secret through surprise (and force, we might add, thinking of the Vicomte) or from willing cooperation (the case of the Marquise, which we shall discuss later):

> Vous avez, il est vrai, le secret de Mlle de Volanges; mais permettez-moi de le dire, je suis autorisé à croire que c'est l'effet de la surprise, et non de la confiance. (Letter 64, p. 131)

Just as Danceny progresses in the course of the novel from the naive innocent who can only "make eyes" at Cécile to the more sophisticated gallant flirting with the Marquise, so too does he advance in sophistication as a reader. The final reason he proposes for his refusal to return Cécile's letters touches on the essential condition implicit in any communication, be it epistolary or amorous:

> Je respecte vos droits, mais ils ne vont pas jusqu'à me dispenser de mes devoirs. Le plus sacré de tous est de ne jamais trahir la confiance qu'on nous accorde. Ce serait y manquer que d'exposer aux yeux d'un autre les secrets d'un cœur qui n'a voulu les dévoiler qu'aux miens. (Letter 64, p. 131)

Danceny's moral rationale provides a perfect literary explanation of the reader's power and of the immorality implicit in being a secret reader. Any extraneous reader, which is to say any reader other than the addressee, the person to whom the letter is addressed and for whom it is intended, disturbs the confidential relationship of speaker and listener because he can learn personal information through this intrusion and then exploit it for his own purposes. Once again it is the novel itself, through the words of one of its own characters, which reminds us of the intimate connection between the content of this story, love and confidence, sex and seduction, and its formal structure as seen in the potential perversion of any communication by hidden and secret readers.

Danceny is not able to provide a solution to the dangers posed by the hidden reader. It is not accidental that Danceny's comments, as well as the specific terms he employs, i.e., *confiance, secrets,* reinforce what we have already said about mutual confidence and trust as well as the dangers of betrayal. His words serve, then, as a warning for that dangerous area where secret readers like the Vicomte de Valmont and the Marquise de Merteuil read and thereby dominate others.

We turn now to the Marquise de Merteuil who, like Valmont, can be an invisible and hidden reader. Like him, she uses her position as the reader of other people's letters to advance her own libertine projects. What distinguishes her from the Vicomte, however, is that while he becomes a secret reader by force and violence, or, in his own words, by *autorité,* she obtains her listening position from the consent of the narrator, which is an instance of *finesse.* Valmont exploits what we might call the typically male characteristic of brute strength. The Marquise chooses the much more difficult and demanding alternative of imposing herself and her presence as hidden reader with the cooperation of the narrator. Being a hidden reader is not only the point at which Valmont and Merteuil most resemble each other, since they both exploit the power inherent in this covert and secret reader for their libertine purposes, but also the point at which they most diverge, since each one is also a very different kind of concealed listener.

The Invited Intruder: Mme de Merteuil

The Marquise de Merteuil is, along with Valmont, one of the two principal libertines in this novel. She equals him in the immorality of her conduct and perhaps surpasses him in the relentless and cold-blooded execution of her licentious projects. To be such a paragon, even of evil, is no small accomplishment. More impressive is the fact that Merteuil is a woman who excels at what is usually considered a man's game.[6] Playing the seductive rake and the licentious rogue is a man's role, while the woman is supposed to be more passive, always on the defensive as she resists her seducer's attack. How can we explain, then, the Marquise's extraordinary success as a (male) libertine? In my view, Mme de Merteuil's triumphs derive from her very astute use of the advantages of reading. She succeeds as a libertine because she is an expert hidden or secret reader.

There can be no doubt that Mme de Merteuil is a self-possessed woman of iron will, determination, and intelligence:

> Mais moi, qu'ai-je de commun avec ces femmes inconsidérées? Quand m'avez-vous vue m'écarter des règles que je me suis prescrites et manquer à mes principes? . . . ils

sont le fruit de mes profondes réflexions; je les ai créés, et je puis dire que je suis mon ouvrage. (Letter 81, p. 175)

In her social milieu as well as in the libertine activities she has chosen to undertake, she must be able to hide her strength and intelligence and appear different from what she really is: "Cette utile curiosité, en servant à m'instruire, m'apprit encore à dissimuler" (letter 81, p. 175). To conceal herself and her innermost thoughts is a necessary protection that she will eventually turn into power. But first she dissembles:

> je n'avais à moi que ma pensée, et je m'indignais qu'on pût me la ravir ou me la surprendre contre ma volonté. . . . non contente de ne plus me laisser pénétrer, je m'amusais à me montrer sous des formes différentes. (Letter 81, p. 175)

Thus she determines to acquire through a course of study she designs for herself a strategy both to conceal her own thoughts and to divine those of others. It is significant that the material she studies is primarily literary:

> je voyais pourtant que, pour y parvenir, il suffisait de joindre à l'esprit d'un auteur, le talent d'un comédien. Je m'exerçai dans les deux genres, et peut-être avec quelque succès: mais au lieu de rechercher les vains applaudissements du théâtre, je résolus d'employer à mon bonheur ce que tant d'autres sacrifiaient à la vanité. (Letter 81, p. 178)

To become a powerful, active, and independent agent seeking her own pleasure and her own fate, free of the social constraints that hampered her female contemporaries, the Marquise joins to the *esprit d'un auteur,* that is, her function as a narrator and writer of letters, her *talent d'un comédien,* or her role as reader. For to be an outstanding reader requires an accomplished actress's theatrical talent for disguising truth, creating illusions, and appearing to be what she is not.

The apparent reader is the person to whom the letter is addressed even though other, unintended recipients may also read it. Reading, especially of the second variety, is critical, since it determines very often the real meaning, the deep significance that a letter possesses. In other words, we can say that a letter's meaning is fixed only when we know who reads it: our interpretation, as readers of the entire novel, is determined in part by our knowledge of which characters in the novel have access to and read various letters. One of the clearest illustrations of the power of the reader to change meanings and thus to establish new interpretations is found in letter 48, which Valmont writes to the Présidente de Tourvel, whom he is trying to seduce:

> C'est après une nuit orageuse, et pendant laquelle je n'ai pas fermé l'œil; c'est après avoir été sans cesse ou dans l'agitation d'une ardeur dévorante, ou dans l'entier

> anéantissement de toutes les facultés de mon âme, que je viens chercher auprès de vous, Madame, un calme dont j'ai besoin, et dont pourtant je n'espère pas pouvoir jouir encore. . . . Quoi! ne puis-je donc espérer que vous partagerez quelque jour le trouble que j'éprouve en ce moment? (Letter 48, p. 100)

We know that Valmont is a rake and that he has decided to attack Mme de Tourvel. But we cannot appreciate the precise meanings of every phrase in this apparently touching and perhaps unctuous letter unless we also know that Valmont has already sent a copy to the Marquise and explained to her how another lady friend of his, of very easy virtue, had served

> de pupitre pour écrire à ma belle dévote, à qui j'ai trouvé plaisant d'envoyer une lettre écrite du lit et presque dans les bras d'une fille, interrompue même pour une infidélité complète, et dans laquelle je lui rendis un compte exact de ma situation et de ma conduite. (Letter 47, p. 99)

Merteuil's power as reader is precisely that she gives this apparently loving and longing letter its true meaning, its full libertine sense: Valmont is mocking the Présidente with his ambiguous phrases and his concealed allusions. When he writes, for example,

> Jamais je n'eus tant de plaisir en vous écrivant; jamais je ne ressentis, dans cette occupation, une émotion si douce, et cependant si vive. (Letter 48, p. 101)

Mme de Tourvel will interpret this as a lover's hyperbole. Merteuil's reading differs drastically. For her the term *read* is to be taken in both senses: the act of reading she is performing on this letter as well as the (different!) interpretation that her reading produces. As sardonic as it is, this letter delivers its full impact only when we reflect upon this double reading and upon the gap separating the first reader from the second. Valmont's cruelty is less in his words than in the discrepancy between his performance and his intention. The latter can only be inferred, but it is nonetheless frightening because we are free to imagine the depths of the Vicomte's perversity. The unspoken, lying in the interface of these two letters, these two readers, and their two readings of that single letter, implies more than can be said. In a real sense, Valmont has written this letter on Emilie through Tourvel to Merteuil: she is his true addressee, the person to whom the real message is directed. Valmont wants to prove something to the Marquise, he is attempting to convince her that he does not love the Présidente but merely wants to seduce and abandon her. To the extent that Valmont feels an obligation to explain himself to the Marquise, to convince her that what he is saying and doing is sufficiently libertine, to that extent Mme de Merteuil exerts power over him, a power that resides literally in her position as reader, as the true although hidden addressee of this letter.

At the very center of his novel, Laclos offers us an example of readerly power and manipulation. As the narrator of letter 87, the Marquise demonstrates her own fine awareness of the importance of reading and of how reading can become a strategy and a weapon in the world of libertine intrigue. Rich with her own experience as a reader, Merteuil as narrator is able to maneuver her own readers while she avoids being manipulated in her turn. Indeed, the Marquise's expert knowledge of her readers and her consequent ability to control their reading derive from her own experiences as a secret reader in the correspondence between Valmont and Tourvel as well as in the Cécile-Danceny letters. Letter 87 shows how the simple fact of reading belongs to the art of seduction which is, after all, the subject of this novel.

This letter is written by the Marquise to Mme de Volanges and recounts the public version of her encounter with the Marquis de Prévan. It presents the Marquise as an unfortunate victim and Prévan as an unprincipled scoundrel whose unilateral plan to seduce the Marquise is thwarted by the lucky intervention of the latter's servants. According to Merteuil, Prévan had hidden in her bedroom after pretending to leave a late-evening gathering at her home. His intention was, apparently, to force himself upon her as she prepared for bed. What interests us for the moment is the status both of the immediate reader and of the eventual readers of letter 87. Mme de Merteuil assumes that Mme de Volanges *fera lecture publique* of this story, thus making all those present at the château, namely Valmont, Mme de Rosemonde, Cécile Volanges, and Mme de Tourvel, secondary listeners or eventual readers. As such, they will learn indirectly but certainly the Marquise's version of the Prévan incident. They thus become part of the public revulsion and outcry that punish Prévan. They feel outrage at his behavior and they sympathize with the Marquise in her tribulation. Of course, Merteuil is furnishing a doctored version of these events. Her letter offers a falsified account of this incident which simultaneously condemns Prévan as a lecher and libertine while it embellishes her own reputation as an honest and irreproachable woman. We know what really happened, as does Valmont, because we have read letter 85, in which the Marquise gave Valmont a true account of these events. Just as she had cleverly arranged the scene in the bedroom so that Prévan would be discovered in a situation that compromised him but not herself, and thereby aroused public opinion in Paris against him and for herself, so too has the Marquise composed her letter to elicit the reaction she wants from all her readers, who include both the one to whom it is addressed, Mme de Volanges, and the others to whom the latter will read it. Merteuil wants this private letter to become public, she intends its personal message to be general, she is counting upon being read by readers to whom she has not written. Her purpose is to direct these other readers, these superfluous listeners, into accepting her false version of the incident as the true one. Her letter to the château is just as successful as her staging of events in her home and the subsequent propaganda coup she scores in the Parisian gossip circles.

However, we should note several points about Merteuil's exploitation of her readers. Obviously, these secondary addressees are not secret ones since the Marquise plans on them right from the outset and directs her letter as much to them (perhaps even more so) as to its nominal addressee. She wants to influence them and to win their support, which is crucial in the battle of opinions and versions that she is waging against Prévan simultaneously in Paris. Both stratagems work: the Marquise wins the sympathy of the entire Parisian public as well as that of the château. That latter victory is won in written and epistolary terms, and for us it is much more important than the former since it is the only one fully presented in the novel, the only one realized within the fiction rather than simply mentioned. Merteuil's victory by letter demonstrates how important readers are: they control interpretation, they constitute public opinion. In the world of the libertine and his, or her, ruthless campaign of seduction, public opinion is the only counterbalancing force, the only positive opposing virtue, as fragile and precarious as it may be. To control public opinion and to influence what others believe is the ultimate power and the ultimate seduction that a libertine can perform.

This lesson in the manipulation of readers occurs precisely in the middle of the novel, the eighty-seventh letter out of a total of one hundred seventy-five. A key episode in the novel, an echo and reflection on a smaller scale of other seductions and deceptions, this letter illustrates the formidable talents of the Marquise de Merteuil as a rake and seducer. Moreover, it offers a most effective demonstration of indirect power and control, since it shows that the Marquise can foresee and calculate the impact of her epistles on even her most distant and remote readers. Other narrators are less sure in their grasp of the power to tell. But then Mme de Merteuil is also an accomplished listener, a reader of the first rank, and doubtless her prowess in one area has aided her in the other.

As a reader, Mme de Merteuil enjoys two different perspectives. In other words, her readerly activity takes on two different forms. First, she is Valmont's intimate correspondent, the specific individual to whom he addresses thirty-three out of the total of fifty-one letters that he writes in the novel. As his private reader, Merteuil is privy to the secret details that he reveals only to her. She is his intimate receiver, the one to whom he confides his most personal secrets. She capitalizes on this privilege by criticizing constantly his seduction of Mme de Tourvel. She complains, for example, that too often he is not sufficiently aggressive or audacious in his conduct:

> Votre conduite est un chef-d'œuvre de prudence. Elle en serait un de sottise dans la supposition contraire; et, pour vous parler vrai, je crains que vous ne vous fassiez illusion. (Letter 33, p. 66)

She observes caustically that he has become truly enamored of his victim:

> Or, est-il vrai, Vicomte, que vous vous faites illusion sur le sentiment qui vous attache à Mme de Tourvel? C'est de l'amour, ou il n'en exista jamais: vous le niez bien de cent façons; mais vous le prouvez de mille. (Letter 134, p. 318)

She demeans his skill as rake and rogue by pretending that he is lucky in his seductions rather than clever, adroit, or intelligent:

> Vous avez séduit, perdu même beaucoup de femmes: mais quelles difficultés avez-vous eues à vaincre? quels obstacles à surmonter? où est là le mérite qui soit véritablement à vous? Une belle figure, pur effet du hasard; des grâces, que l'usage donne presque toujours; de l'esprit à la vérité, mais auquel du jargon suppléerait au besoin; une impudence assez louable, mais peut-être uniquement due à la facilité de vos premiers succès; si je ne me trompe, voilà tous vos moyens: car pour la célébrité que vous avez pu acquérir, vous n'exigerez pas, je crois, que je compte pour beaucoup l'art de faire naître ou de saisir l'occasion d'un scandale. (Letter 81, pp. 172-73)

Secondly, the Marquise de Merteuil is Valmont's reader in another, less obvious manner, which we have already observed operating in Valmont's ironic message written to Mme de Tourvel while he was in bed with Emilie. Merteuil is an eavesdropper in all of Valmont's letters to Mme de Tourvel. She reads their entire correspondence, ensconced in their supposed private and intimate exchange as a secret reader. It is this status as secondary, supplementary, and hidden reader that confers on her the enormous power she wields from beginning to end of this novel and which she eventually will use against the Vicomte. Throughout his correspondence with Mme de Tourvel, Valmont allows the Marquise to be a supplementary reader, without the knowledge of his immediate reader, the Présidente, to whom he actually addresses these letters. By voluntarily submitting the letters written for the Présidente to Merteuil's scrutiny, Valmont makes a strategic mistake that will have fatal consequences for him. In a sense, he acknowledges her ascendancy over him by permitting her to listen in on his letters to Mme de Tourvel. By making her his secret additional reader, he gives her the formidable weapons that she will finally turn against him. What is most significant is that Valmont confers this power on the Marquise willingly, freely submitting his letters to her. He seems unaware of the potential strength of a hidden reader, while Merteuil is entirely cognizant of its advantages. Valmont's defeat is a direct result of his vulnerability regarding his secret reader. It is almost literally correct to say that Valmont's death takes place at the hands[7] of Merteuil, since she gave Danceny the letters which inspired the latter to provoke the fatal duel. Valmont's downfall can be traced directly to this first mistake concerning his reader and to his failure to recognize the power of reading.

We can see quite clearly in letters 47 and 48 how the supplementary, hidden reader usurps the role of the original addressee and displaces her and her original reading. That second, secret reader understands fully and accurately the intention of the writer while the immediate reader stops at the superficial meaning of the text. Thus, Mme de Tourvel takes quite literally Valmont's amorous exaggerations and sees only the apparent sense of his words:

> l'air que je respire est brûlant de volupté; la table même sur laquelle je vous écris, consacrée pour la première fois à cet usage, devient pour moi l'autel sacré de l'amour; combien elle va s'embellir à mes yeux! j'aurai tracé sur elle le serment de vous aimer toujours! (Letter 48, p. 101)

In contrast, Mme de Merteuil reads the truth behind these deceptive terms and understands fully the cruel, ironic, and libertine joke that Valmont is playing on the Présidente: the voluptuousness is due to Valmont's orgy, the table is Emilie's back, and his claims of excitement and fatigue are the consequences not of his writing but his fornication. Merteuil's very presence as a secret reader, for whose benefit Valmont is showing off his libertine behavior, makes most explicit the fraud and deception underlying everything Valmont says to Mme de Tourvel. Although he offers a plausible excuse for making the Marquise his indirect reader, he is really asking for her approval:

> Comme il faut que ma lettre soit timbrée de Paris, je vous l'envoie; je la laisse ouverte. Vous voudrez bien la lire, la cacheter, et la faire mettre à la poste. (Letter 47, pp. 99-100)

As a rake, Valmont needs someone of equal stature and capacity to appreciate his various projects and especially this attack on Mme de Tourvel. Because seductions like these have less to do with sexual appetites and physical gratification than with self-validation and self-glorification, Valmont wants a kindred soul to watch him and to recognize the professional skill that he brings to his task. The symmetry of the libertine pair Valmont and Merteuil is doubled by the structural opposition of writer and reader: he who speaks must have an equal in whom he can confide and find a mirror image of himself. Earlier, we showed how Merteuil and Valmont were equals and sought peer recognition in their mutual exchanges. There they were apparent readers for each other, the ones to whom they directly addressed and intended their letters; here, the Marquise is a hidden reader and not the intended addressee. This duplicity troubles their bonds of sharing and confidence. The falsification inherent in Merteuil's role as the concealed reader of Mme de Tourvel's letters cannot but contaminate her relationship to Valmont. Thus, each level of (re)reading complicates the situation and alters previous interpretations.

As the secret reader beyond the obvious addressee to whom the letter is sent, the Marquise de Merteuil controls Valmont's perception of himself. Just as she gave the true meaning to letter 48, so too does she give back to Valmont an acceptable and flattering image of himself. Rather, this is what Valmont wants her to do. By withholding this validation, Merteuil exercises a tremendous power over him. The gigantic struggle between Valmont and Merteuil which grows slowly throughout the novel to culminate in his fatal duel with Danceny and her triple loss of beauty, law suit, and reputation, is most clearly articulated through Merteuil's role as a secret reader. Ultimately, the victory will go to the reader who is more hidden and therefore better able to dominate the writer whose letters she is reading.

Examples of Valmont's continual references to sending the Marquise copies of his letters intended for and addressed to the Présidente are almost too numerous to cite. They stand out especially in this novel where such mundane and practical details are most often ignored. For us, however, these reminders are invaluable because they confirm Valmont's desire to have the Marquise as a secret indirect reader of his letters:

> Je joins à ce récit le brouillon de mes deux lettres; vous serez aussi instruite que moi. Si vous voulez être au courant de cette correspondance, il faut vous accoutumer à déchiffrer mes minutes: car pour rien au monde, je ne dévorerais l'ennui de les recopier. (Letter 34, p. 71)

In sharp contrast to Valmont, the Marquise strives to escape the power that she knows every reader possesses. As much as she can, she avoids giving anything remotely compromising to her readers. True, she does send Valmont an accurate and revealing account of her encounter with Prévan as well as an extended biographical sketch of intellectual and (im)moral formation. She does this out of pride, because her rapid and brilliant success with Prévan overshadows Valmont's slow progress with Mme de Tourvel. This failure to follow her strict principles will suffice to destroy her in the end: a single lapse or miscalculation on the Marquise's part about her reader will turn out to be catastrophic.

In that letter in which she gave the true version of the incident with Prévan, we clearly hear Merteuil boasting about her libertine triumphs and implicitly deriding Valmont for his notable lack of success. Just as Valmont needed Merteuil's appreciation and approbation of his conduct, so too does the Marquise use him for the same kind of validation of herself:

> Enfin vous serez tranquille, et surtout vous me rendrez justice. Ecoutez, et ne me confondez plus avec les autres femmes. J'ai mis à fin mon aventure avec Prévan; à fin! entendez-vous bien ce que cela veut dire? A présent vous allez juger qui de lui ou de moi pourra se vanter. Le récit ne sera pas si plaisant que l'action. (Letter 85, p. 188)

This account differs in all important particulars from the public version which she is preparing to send to Mme de Volanges for broadcast, as it were, at the château:

> C'est à ma solitude que vous devez cette longue lettre. J'en écrirai une à Mme de Volanges, dont sûrement elle fera lecture publique, et où vous verrez cette histoire telle qu'il faut la raconter. (Letter 85, p. 197)

While Valmont's seduction of the Présidente requires many letters, Merteuil devotes only one to her struggle with Prévan. Even though the Marquise does write two versions of the Prévan incident, one for Mme de Volanges and one for Valmont, they are mutually exclusive. At the end of the novel, when the private version is made public and read by everyone, it eclipses and entirely replaces that first public account. From the point of view of Merteuil's fictional readers, there is always but one version. Mme de Volanges never suspects the truth behind her false account, while Valmont never doubts the accuracy of his version. The Marquise sends her approved version(s) of the facts only after the action is terminated. Her readers can never evaluate her behavior even in terms of her own predictions because she never leaves any traces. Her self-contained account, which places the entire incident in a past tense over which she has absolute control, prevents Valmont from judging or criticizing her while she is attacking Prévan. In contrast, Valmont remains the butt of her criticisms because his relationship to the Présidente is an ongoing one, in a present tense he cannot hope to master completely, and because he has provided her with a special viewpoint as his secret reader in all his letters to Mme de Tourvel. Her single letter avoids giving him a similar advantage. By adopting this *fait accompli* attitude, she effectively denies him the opportunity to second guess her, a tactic that she enjoys and exploits so readily as his secondary and supplementary reader. When she reports her victory, she can at the same time expose her strategy since she knows it has already succeeded. By concentrating what could have been a prolonged account into one letter, Merteuil demonstrates her reluctance to open herself to an intimate reader, even when that reader is her old friend and confidant Valmont. One further indication of that reluctance to have any reader, even the (for the moment) trusted Valmont, is contained in that final phrase: "Le récit ne sera pas si plaisant que l'action." The Marquise wants to tell this story because it so enhances her reputation and shows her as superior to the Vicomte. Nonetheless, she cannot overcome entirely her reservations about the dangers of being read. She therefore declares her preference for an action which leaves no traces and cannot be read over a written account whose inherent danger is that it may be read by unwanted readers whose very act of reading threatens the author. Merteuil is caught here in a paradox: she must write about this adventure to make it real and to reap its rewards, and yet she is afraid (and rightfully so) of the consequences that writing and reading necessarily entail.

This wary distrust and refusal to be at ease with any reader, no matter how remote or removed, complement perfectly Merteuil's mastery of the libertine code of behavior. Her delight in Prévan's defeat at his own game, which is of course Valmont's game, too, stems in part from her desire to provoke the latter's praise and admiration:

> Cependant, si vous avez quelque grand coup à faire, si vous devez tenter quelque entreprise où ce rival dangereux vous paraissait à craindre, arrivez. Il vous laisse le champ libre, au moins pour quelque temps; peut-être même ne se relèvera-t-il jamais du coup que je lui ai porté. . . . Je vous le demande, qu'eussiez-vous fait de mieux? (Letter 85, pp. 189, 191)

More important, this is a challenge, a feat of libertinage that she dares him to equal or surpass: "qu'eussiez-vous fait de mieux?" Since Valmont was never her secret reader, that is to say an intrusive judge and spying critic for her even though she has been one for him, she knows that he can never denigrate her victory over Prévan while she can always find fault with him on his handling of the Présidente. In this struggle between writer and reader, Mme de Merteuil has the upper hand. Valmont attempts to argue his way out of his weak position, but he fails to convince us that he is doing more than disguising his spite:

> Je parie bien que, depuis votre aventure, vous attendez chaque jour mes compliments et mes éloges; je ne doute même pas que vous n'ayez pris un peu d'humeur de mon long silence; mais que voulez-vous? j'ai toujours pensé que quand il n'y avait plus que des louanges à donner à une femme, on pouvait s'en reposer sur elle, et s'occuper d'autre chose. (Letter 96, p. 213)

Further on, he defends his own tactics for seduction against the Marquise's strategy:

> Ce n'est pas de Mme de Tourvel que je veux vous parler; sa marche trop lente vous déplaît. Vous n'aimez que les affaires faites. Les scènes filées vous ennuient; et moi, jamais je n'avais goûté le plaisir que j'éprouve dans ces lenteurs prétendues.
> Oui, j'aime à voir, à considérer cette femme prudente, engagée, sans s'en être aperçue, dans un sentier qui ne permet plus de retour, et dont la pente rapide et dangereuse l'entraîne malgré elle, et la force à me suivre. . . . Ah! laissez-moi du moins le temps d'observer ces touchants combats entre l'amour et la vertu! (Letter 96, pp. 213-14)

Despite such protestations, Valmont remains vulnerable to the Marquise's censure whenever his projects do not turn out exactly as he expected. He, on the other hand, never knows the Marquise's designs until they are completed. As narrator, Valmont speaks in the present and plans for the future, knowing that his projects may be thwarted; as reader, Merteuil enjoys a retrospective command over the written word and the past and fashions them both to suit her own purposes.

Mme de Merteuil is quite aware that her power as a reader depends on a very delicate balance of factors whose equilibrium she must constantly maintain. These factors echo the principal stages of her self-education and her personal adjustments to society, which she detailed in her so-called autobiographical letter to Valmont (letter 81, quoted in part above). Principally, she relies on secrecy and invisibility. Her presence as an extra reader in all of Valmont's letters to Mme de Tourvel has to remain a secret from the other readers in the text and especially from the Présidente herself. Furthermore, to complement this invisibility she attains as a reader, Merteuil as a writer must avoid being read by others as much as possible. That statement is not a contradiction in terms. It means that she tries at all costs to avoid having any reader other than the single one to whom she specifically addresses her letter. The letters which she does allow, and indeed intends, others to read, like the letter to Mme de Volanges at the château, are careful performances that never compromise her. Her letter about Prévan is nothing but a device to protect herself while damaging him. She even goes so far as to burn a note which Prévan slipped to her one evening. Furthermore, she points out that in so doing she was only following her usual prudent procedure. Even in so minor a detail, the Marquise takes precautions so that no one will be able to find and read this note and thereby fathom the complex deviousness of her plot. Merteuil intends to frustrate any potentially hostile readers by not leaving any traces, any letters, any indications that might belie the report she has circulated about Prévan's motives and intentions. Merteuil is similarly guarded in her seductions of other men. The letter which invites Belleroche to a night of pleasure with the Marquise is surrounded by mystery. It is delivered by Merteuil's maid, Victoire, disguised as a footman, while the rendezvous itself is indicated in a "billet de moi, mais non de mon écriture, suivant ma prudente règle" (letter 10, p. 27). This ever-present fear of leaving traces which an unintended reader might interpret to her disadvantage has prompted the Marquise to adhere strictly to a fundamental rule concerning both writing and her libertine behavior. She formulates this principle in her autobiographical letter 81, where she explains a good deal about her intellectual and (im)moral education as well as about her innate fear of unintended readers:

> Ces précautions et celles de ne jamais écrire, de ne livrer jamais aucune preuve de ma défaite, pouvaient paraître excessives, et ne m'ont jamais paru suffisantes. (Letter 81, p. 179)

From her own experience as an intrusive reader, she knows that the last reading determines the complete meaning of any letter. Merteuil's intuition about the dangers of reading and of having unwanted readers explains the difference between her and Valmont. He constantly exposes himself to her jibes and invidious comparisons by giving her so much evidence of his contact, and especially of his failures, with Mme de Tourvel, while the Marquise does not afford him any similar opportunities. She hides her activities as best she can, preferring to reveal them in one finished and "perfected" version that cannot be questioned. It will require only a single mistake, one or two misguided letters, in order to imperil, indeed to destroy, the Marquise's carefully nurtured reputation. We must always remember that the Marquise is a woman and that, in her time and place, her "right" to do wrong is neither as secure nor as accepted as Valmont's or Prévan's. Her desire, so unusual in a woman, to be fully the equal of any male libertine harbors a profoundly dangerous threat for the male-dominated society around her.[8] Consequently, she runs a special risk because she dares to consider herself equal to and even better than men. The menace that the Marquise can see in any unintended reader reflects in part her unusual situation as a female rake as well as the hypocritical societal reaction which condones in the male what it so strongly reproves and punishes in the female. Of all the characters in the novel only Merteuil is fully conscious of the power of reading, which her own downfall illustrates perfectly. Given this danger which the Marquise can always perceive on the horizon, we better appreciate her efforts to cover her tracks, to leave no traces for subsequent readers.

The Marquise's deliberate care in erasing any evidence of her activity as a libertine and any trace of her presence as a secret listener or hidden reader in others' correspondences continues in her efforts to conceal the tracks she has left as a writer. On at least one occasion she reminds Valmont to conceal the proof of her corrupting influence upon Cécile. That damning evidence is nothing more than a letter she wrote to Cécile:

> Ce parti que je crois le meilleur, et auquel je me suis arrêtée, m'a décidée à mener la jeune personne un peu vite, comme vous verrez par ma lettre; il rend aussi très important de ne rien laisser entre ses mains qui puisse me compromettre, et je vous prie d'y avoir attention. Cette précaution une fois prise, je me charge du moral. (Letter 106, p. 249)

The Marquise knows full well that the advantage she enjoys over Valmont is that she can eavesdrop on his letters to the Présidente. Should anyone do that to her letters to Cécile, she would be placed in a similar position of inferiority and helplessness. She takes precautions therefore to eliminate the very possibility of any subsequent and unwanted readers. Just as she burned Prévan's note, here she repossesses the physical evidence, the letter itself which connects her to Cécile. In both cases, the potentially incriminating items are letters, written words that can be read. The very nature of the traces that can implicate the Marquise underlines the real significance of the reader in this novel.

In the end, Merteuil is defeated precisely by this unwanted and unintended reader whom she has always feared and whom she has valiantly but in vain tried to escape. The very same letters which established the high-water mark of her libertine conduct also contain the seeds of her defeat. Merteuil fails to control completely the ultimate reading of letter 85, which contains the true account of the Prévan incident, and letter 81, her autobiographical sketch. These failures to control her ultimate and unforeseen readers cause her downfall.

Immediately after their duel, Danceny and Valmont come to some sort of understanding. Despite their quarrel, they do establish a real bond of personal affection. As proof of their new friendship, the dying Valmont gives Danceny the entire correspondence he has had with the Marquise. It is to avenge Valmont as much as himself that Danceny publishes those two letters which are most dangerous from Merteuil's point of view. This scene is described by M. Bertrand, the family lawyer, in his letter to Mme de Rosemonde. Bertrand focuses our attention on the transfer of Merteuil's letters and the imminence of their finding new readers. He describes in detail how

> M. le vicomte s'est montré bien véritablement grand. Il m'a ordonné de me taire; et celui-là même, qui était son meurtrier, il lui a pris la main, l'a appelé son ami, l'a embrassé. . . . Il lui a, de plus, fait remettre, devant moi, des papiers fort volumineux, que je ne connais pas, mais auxquels je sais bien qu'il attachait beaucoup d'importance. (Letter 163, pp. 371-72)

Merteuil's loss of control over who shall be her readers is made explicit by Danceny when he writes to Mme de Rosemonde:

> N'en croyez pas mes discours; mais lisez, si vous en avez le courage, la correspondance que je dépose entre vos mains. La quantité de lettres qui s'y trouvent en original paraît rendre authentiques celles dont il n'existe que des copies. Au reste, j'ai reçu ces papiers, tels que j'ai l'honneur de vous les adresser, de M. de Valmont lui-même. Je n'y ai rien ajouté, et je n'en ai distrait que deux Lettres que je me suis permis de publier. (Letter 169, p. 382)

To publish letters that were intended to remain intimate and private is of course to upset any expectation regarding their addressees because it introduces into the narrative structure a whole new set of readers. These new readers are of course critics and judges, precisely the kind of reader the Marquise has constantly attempted to avoid. Danceny's imperative *lisez* is meant most literally. It is an invitation that opens the text to new readings, it is a command that brings into the communication circuit readers who are unwanted as far as the Marquise is concerned. Reading is the act that avenges both Valmont and Danceny, that forms and informs public opinion, and that precipitates Merteuil's downfall. Reading is therefore a most powerful verb, just as the one who reads is a most powerful figure.

Unfortunately for the Marquise, her ultimate readers are legion: everyone in Paris wants to read the Marquise's two most personal and compromising letters. Her most intimate confessions become most public knowledge. That is the defeat that Merteuil suffers, and it strikes her in her strength, in the very essence of her libertine character. She who was herself the most secret reader and the most concealed writer has finally been revealed and unmasked by the very act of reading that formerly assured her success as a rake.

Significantly, the revised public opinion about the Marquise is first reported by Mme de Volanges, who was the vehicle Merteuil chose to broadcast her own version of the Prévan incident:

> On dit donc que la querelle survenue entre M. de Valmont et le chevalier Danceny est l'ouvrage de Mme de Merteuil qui les trompait également tous deux ... et que pour achever de faire connaître Mme de Merteuil au chevalier Danceny, et aussi pour se justifier entièrement, M. de Valmont a joint à ses discours une foule de lettres, formant une correspondance régulière qu'il entretenait avec elle, et où celle-ci raconte sur elle-même, et dans le style le plus libre, les anecdotes les plus scandaleuses. (Letter 168, p. 379)

The most important consequence of Danceny's publication of these letters is that the Marquise loses her privileged position of having no other personage who reads her private letters. Now everyone can read her letters, everyone knows her secret. That is the tremendous force in Danceny's injunction to Mme de Rosemonde: *lisez*! Notice also that in the words of Danceny and Mme de Volanges themselves, a capital distinction is made between *discours*, vain words which leave no traces, and *lettres*, written documents that can be (re)read and interpreted in ways that the writer might not have intended. Thanks to such traces and the reevaluations they produce, everyone learns the true facts behind the Prévan scandal. The secret letter she had written to Valmont gave the correct version of the situation. For lack of sufficient readers, however, it did not form (and inform) public opinion, as did the other letter which was false but read and made public by Mme de Volanges. Now the situation is reversed because many new readers are reading that once secret letter. Having many readers, being published, and coming to the attention of the public are all devices or metaphors for getting at the truth. In Mme de Volanges's words:

> Voici ce qu'on publie; ou, pour mieux dire, ce qu'on murmure encore, mais qui ne tardera sûrement pas à éclater davantage. (Letter 168, p. 379)

Even when presented with the evidence, Mme de Volanges is not entirely convinced that the Marquise has done wrong. However she was not at all perceptive regarding her own daughter, Cécile, so it is not surprising that she should be fooled again about her friend the Marquise. Still she does describe that letter

> qui justifie entièrement M. de Prévan, dont vous vous rappelez l'histoire, par la preuve qui s'y trouve qu'il n'a fait au contraire que céder aux avances les plus marquées de Mme de Merteuil, et que le rendez-vous était convenu avec elle. (Letter 168, p. 379)

The Marquise is defeated in the end by the very weapons that she has used against others. In purely literary and structural terms, Merteuil's defeat comes in the form of these unwanted readers who intrude into the private space of her correspondence and who were totally unforeseen when she wrote these letters. The other signs of her downfall (catching smallpox, losing her lawsuit, going bankrupt, and finally self-imposed exile) belong to the realm of plot and intrigue. Their justification and internal logic, however, stem from Merteuil's relationship to her unwanted readers.

Despite the power that the Marquise de Merteuil wields as a reader, at the end of this novel she is defeated. Critics have long objected to this denouement which, they feel, is artificial and only perfunctorily moral.[9] But Mme de Merteuil's setback is in no way inappropriate or illogical, since it depends on the very principles of the Marquise's own success: the power of reading and the awareness of one's readers. Her defeat takes place entirely in terms of discourse, while Valmont's death, in a duel, is more extraneous to this literary universe of the written word and of letters. Mme de Merteuil succeeds and eventually fails in purely literary terms. The source of her strength as well as the cause of her upset are both implicit in the very narrative act that underlies the whole epistolary novel and in the writing/reading activity which almost displaces sexual seduction as the novel's true center.

Both Valmont and Merteuil show themselves to be masters of reading and experts at the difficult task of becoming secret readers. This similarity should not disguise the real differences between them, however. What Valmont accomplishes by bribery, blackmail, intimidation, and theft, the Marquise does with the cooperation and the compliance of one of the participants. As Merteuil cleverly seduces Danceny, she makes a most perceptive comment about her privileged position as a reader even though she is ostensibly talking about her social relationship with Cécile and the Chevalier. Danceny is dreaming of keeping both Cécile and the Marquise as friends, lovers, and readers:

> en sorte que quand vous serez, je suppose, auprès de votre maîtresse, vous ne sauriez pas y vivre que je n'y sois en tiers. (Letter 121, p. 284)

As a *secret* third party: Merteuil's great accomplishment both with Danceny and Valmont is to get herself invited, as an outside third party, to listen in on what should be an exclusive two-person exchange. This is the full sense of those terms, *finesse* and *adresse,* which Valmont employed to distinguish the arms of the female sex from his own masculine qualities of strength and *autorité.*

Merteuil's arguable superiority over Valmont as a libertine and her identification as a malevolent, satanic figure derive from the aura of omnipotence which is directly attributable to her activity as a secret reader. As she eavesdrops on others, she inserts herself as a third force into the normally binary exchange of letters. Outside the normal circuit, she is superior to the other participants in it. A master reader, she learns how to manipulate Valmont from his letters to Mme de Tourvel just as she controls Cécile and Danceny through their letters to each other. Whereas Valmont, the active, physical, initiating principle of libertine behavior, dominates the writing of letters (he is the novel's most prolific narrator), Merteuil controls their reading. Thus she embodies a more passive, insinuating—dare we say feminine?—form of licentious consciousness.[10] Clearly, Valmont and Merteuil are a complementary pair, writer and reader, male and female. At another level, nonetheless, they are bitter rivals, each one measuring the other, each one attempting to outdo the other. The entire novel is comprehensible only in this context of binary opposition which pits the Vicomte against the Marquise in alternating episodes of mutual aid and of mutual aggression. Such a dynamic tension is best illustrated, in my opinion, by the symmetrical opposition of their respective triumphs as a strong-arm thief and as an invited intruder.

4

Split Personalities: Characterizing Writers and Readers

As we have already seen, each of the novel's characters has a double function, first that of writing letters or of being a narrator, and second, that of receiving another's letters or of being a reader. This dual function in the structure of the novel corresponds to a double personality profile at the psychological level of characterization, since each personage displays a different aspect of his or her personality according to his or her role as either narrator or reader. Consequently, we can analyze each character in terms of this narrator/reader distinction. In such successful and well-rounded figures as we find in the *Liaisons dangereuses,* this distinction might at first seem arbitrary. Nonetheless, the value of the distinction and of the consequent analysis is real. As subtle as the two faces of each character are, and as difficult as it may be to differentiate precisely between them, the contrast between the very same character as writer and as reader reveals accurately the secret workings of their personalties and demonstrates another subtle element of Laclos's artistry.

Cécile Volanges

Cécile Volanges changes drastically when we compare her personality as narrator to her character as reader. Cécile opens the novel, and her frequent letters at the outset carry a heavy burden of exposition. Of the first twenty letters, she contributes eight, while the remaining twelve are distributed among Valmont, Merteuil, Danceny, Mme de Tourvel, and Mme de Volanges. Critics have commented upon the particular tone of voice[1] that Laclos has given to Cécile's letters and consequently to her personality as narrator: juvenile, ingenuous, garrulous, credulous, disorganized, overly enthusiastic, and easily moved from one emotional height to another. Even her grammatical faults are indications of her unformed intelligence and lack of sophistication. They point up the gap, even if it is for the moment merely linguistic, that separates her from such adepts of word and deed as Valmont and Merteuil. For an admittedly secondary character, Cécile does write a large number of letters, a number that is perhaps disproportionate to her importance in the intrigue, since she writes more than Mme de Tourvel (twenty-five versus twenty-four). Like the latter, Cécile is important as a victim, the prey of Valmont and Merteuil. Nevertheless, she does not capture our interest as a human being as much or as intensely as the Présidente, who is so much more mature and intelligent. Mme de Tourvel is a moving and fascinating woman who rewards our interest with the complexity of her own personality. Cécile is neither as rich nor as deep a character as the Présidente, and consequently she attracts our attention less.

Still, Mlle de Volanges's seduction and fall remain key structural elements, indispensable for the full impact of this depiction of libertine behavior and betrayed innocence. As regards the psychology of the characters, however, Cécile is but a minor figure, filling out the cast but not really permitted to linger in the spotlight. This brief personality sketch, which could be expanded without changing anything essential, is based on Cécile's role as narrator. We have judged her upon what she has written, we have evaluated her in terms of her presence as a producer of letters.

Let us complete our personality sketch by looking now at Cécile as a reader and assessing her as a receiver of letters. Immediately we notice how reduced a character she becomes. While writing twenty-five letters, she receives only eleven. Furthermore, her principal epistolary exchange with Sophie Carnay is severely truncated, cut in half by the elimination of all of Sophie's letters. What Cécile reads and what inspires her to write in her turn do not exist in the novel. Alone of all the personages, Cécile is deprived of the motivations that would be apparent in a two-sided correspondence. She loses the richness of human interest that a written dialogue would supply. Without Sophie and the writer/reader balance she would provide, Cécile remains quite literally without text-ure. Of course, this reduction is a necessary artistic economy, eliminating a possible diversion and concentrating our attention on the principal characters and the main intrigue. Sophie's letters would add nothing to the thrust of the plot and would needlessly encumber the forward impulsion of the action. Despite these self-evident reasons, the editors do feel obliged to explain this omission and in a sense to defend it:

> Pour ne pas abuser de la patience du lecteur, on supprime beaucoup de lettres de cette correspondance journalière, qui à elle seule comprendrait plusieurs volumes, on ne donne que celles qui ont paru nécessaires à l'intelligence des événements de cette société. C'est par le même motif qu'on supprime aussi toutes les lettres de Sophie Carnay et plusieurs de celles des autres acteurs de ces aventures. (Letter 7, note, p. 20)

Cécile has the misfortune to be the victim of this editorial policy on more than one occasion. In a footnote to a reference made by Danceny in one of his letters to Cécile, the editors intervene and explain once again:

> Cette lettre est celle dont Cécile Volanges envoie copie à Madame de Merteuil. Comme elle redit en partie les mêmes choses que les deux précédentes on a cru qu'elle suffisait pour ne pas grossir inutilement ce recueil. (Letter 28, note, p. 59)

And finally, one last deletion:

> On continue de supprimer les lettres de Cécile Volanges et du chevalier Danceny, qui sont peu intéressantes et n'annoncent aucun événement. (Letter 39, note, p. 81)

We have already discussed how these editors belong to the twilight fringe of this fictional universe. They separate or perhaps they connect the fictive world of the novel and the real, eighteenth-century society in which this novel is inscribed and upon which it depends for authenticating support and for a referential background. Laclos's decision to suppress Sophie is artistically correct and the reasons for diminishing Cécile are perfectly sound, since her letters are "not very interesting" and therefore not "necessary." However correct in artistic terms, these suppressions nevertheless do violate the logic of the epistolary genre, which is premised on two-sided exchanges, and the example of the *Liaisons* itself, which grants its other characters this privilege of give-and-take correspondences. This detail does then belong to our consideration of the fictional reader even though it might at first appear meaningless. Not only has the author de-created a fictional reader, but he chooses precisely those ironic, contradictory, and problematic figures, the two editors, to perform this deletion and to justify it.

Because her letters are not reproduced, Sophie does not exist within the text. If Sophie does not exist as a narrator, then Cécile is rendered moot as a reader. Furthermore, Cécile's writerly impact is seriously reduced because as an addresser she is deprived of her addressee, Sophie. Cécile's rank as a secondary or minor character is not therefore a subjective value judgment that compares her unfavorably with the Présidente or that is based on a literary convention concerning the psychology of fictional characters. It is rather a structural fact and the simple consequence of the written record, or rather of the gaps in that written record. Cécile barely exists as a reader while the other characters display a balance or at least a justifiable proportion between their writing and reading functions.

Because of this reduced presence, Cécile reveals most clearly the frontier or boundary where fiction starts and ends. Finding herself in the abnormal position of a writer who has no reader, Cécile defines the point of incision, that cut in the otherwise seamless fabric where the novel's first threads begin. Her deficit as a personality is redeemed by the structural importance she has in the novel's incipit. Her diminished role as a reader (it is principally the nonexistent Sophie who writes to her) allows the fiction to slip into an apparently real world of letters. Reduced to the bare minimum, honed to a razor's edge, Cécile's textual presence/absence, her appearance as narrator juxtaposed to her disappearance as a reader, mark that vanishing point where Laclos hopes to create the illusion of fiction blending into reality, of the fictional world disappearing into the real society which inspired it.

Armed with this analysis, we can now return to our discussion of Cécile's personality and complete the thumbnail sketch that we made of her character based on her activity as a narrator. Psychologically, Mlle de Volanges is the ideal candidate for the structural reduction that losing one's existence as a reader supposes. To refuse her the normal condition of a complete epistolary character, both writer and reader, created in a regular two-way exchange of letters, emphasizes her half-developed intelligence, her inability to adjust successfully to her mother's social milieu, and her own catastrophic efforts to shift for herself and to behave like an adult. Her special vulnerability is prepared by her incompleteness as an addressee and by her unfilled textual relationship with Sophie. Once the novel is beyond its exposition phase, the editors announce that they will even omit the letters Cécile writes to Sophie:

> Mlle de Volanges ayant peu de temps après changé de confidente, comme on le verra par la suite de ces lettres, on ne trouvera plus dans ce recueil aucune de celles qu'elle a continué d'écrire à son amie du couvent: elles n'apprendraient rien au lecteur. (Letter 75, note, p. 153)

Form mirrors content here; the pattern set in the infrastructure parallels that in the plot. Cécile's social and moral naiveté stems from the absence of any sure critera for making sane judgments as well as from the textual absence that surrounds her and isolates her from any possibility of rescue. She is cut adrift from her addressee, and ignored by her mother. Deprived of Sophie's replies and of her mother's attention, Cécile cannot resist the presence of Mme de Merteuil and the response the latter gives her. As her very name indicates, Mlle de Volanges is *volage*, light and flighty because, in part, she lacks the weight and seriousness that being a complete reader would confer upon her. To make a pun which should not however obscure the gravity of this situation, we can go so far as to say that Cécile's textual insufficiency explains her sexual immaturity. Furthermore, since we are dealing here with a novel and not with life, that is to say with a reality that exists only in letters, we can claim that her textual deficiency is in large part responsible for her sexual difficulties.

Mme de Volanges

Mme de Volanges, Cécile's mother, also reveals two distinct personalities according to her activity either as narrator or reader. As a writer of letters,

Split Personalities 85

Mme de Volanges presents herself as a relatively sophisticated, intelligent, and typically correct example of a certain eighteenth-century social class under the *ancien régime*. Her letters to the Présidente de Tourvel exhibit a polish and *savoir-faire* as well as a discerning grasp on the libertine realities of the world she lives in:

> Je n'ai jamais douté, ma jeune et belle amie, ni de l'amitié que vous avez pour moi, ni de l'intérêt sincère que vous prenez à tout ce qui me regarde. . . . Mais Valmont n'est pas cela. Sa conduite est le résultat de ses principes. Il sait calculer tout ce qu'un homme peut se permettre d'horreurs sans se compromettre; et pour être cruel et méchant sans danger, il a choisi les femmes pour victimes. (Letter 9, pp. 22-23)

Her haughty letter to Danceny, which attempts to thwart his incipient romance with Cécile, is eloquent. Its carefully worded demands and threats, its barely disguised outrage, and its willful suppression of personal emotion in favor of a socially acceptable solution indicate that Mme de Volanges is indeed a woman of sense and intelligence, and one who thoroughly comprehends the need for decorum and the respect due to appearances:

> Après avoir abusé, Monsieur, de la confiance d'une mère et de l'innocence d'un enfant, vous ne serez pas surpris, sans doute, de ne plus être reçu dans une maison où vous n'avez répondu aux preuves de l'amitié la plus sincère que par l'oubli de tous les procédés. . . . Je vous préviens aussi que si vous faites à l'avenir la moindre tentative pour entretenir ma fille dans l'égarement où vous l'avez plongée, une retraite austère et éternelle la soustraira à vos poursuites. (Letter 62, p. 123)

Her single letter to the Marquise de Merteuil touches on the pathetic as Mme de Volanges plaintively demands how to react to her daughter's sudden change in demeanor and behavior:

> Quel parti prendre pourtant, si cela dure? ferai-je le malheur de ma fille? tournerai-je contre elle les qualités les plus précieuses de l'âme, la sensibilité et la constance? est-ce pour cela que je suis sa mère? . . . si je force son choix, n'aurai-je pas à répondre des suites funestes qu'il peut avoir? Quel usage à faire de l'autorité maternelle, que de placer sa fille entre le crime et le malheur! (Letter 98, pp. 221-22)

These searching questions ring true. Mme de Volanges is perfectly sincere in trying to resolve this dilemma even though she is addressing the person least apt to help her or her daughter. Finally, Mme de Volanges insists upon remaining faithful to those she considers friends even when the latter fall on hard times. This noble and courageous gesture is somewhat tarnished since the friend in question is none other than the Marquise who has just been shunned by everyone she meets at the theater. Despite our awareness that the Marquise's disgrace is justified, that she has been rightfully unmasked, and that she will now be punished for her immoral conduct, Mme de Volanges's report of Merteuil's fall and Prévan's triumph displays an admirable skepticism about the still unproven rumors circulating in the salons and an acute consciousness of how fickle the public's applause can really be:

> Il se répand ici, ma chère et digne amie, sur le compte de Mme de Merteuil, des bruits bien étonnants et bien fâcheux. Assurément je suis loin d'y croire, et je parierais bien que ce n'est qu'une affreuse calomnie; mais je sais trop combien les méchancetés, même les moins vraisemblables, prennent aisément consistance, et combien l'impression qu'elles laissent s'efface difficilement. . . . J'ai heureusement les plus fortes raisons de croire que ces imputations sont aussi fausses qu'odieuses. . . . Ces réflexions me porteraient à le [i.e., Prévan] soupçonner l'auteur des bruits qui courent aujourd'hui, et à regarder ces noirceurs comme l'ouvrage de sa haine et de sa vengeance, fait dans l'espoir de répandre au moins des doutes, et de causer peut-être une diversion utile. (Letter 168, pp. 378, 379, 380)

Eventually Mme de Volanges sees the truth and understands that the Marquise never deserved her support and fidelity. Nonetheless, in defense of Mme de Volanges, we must admit that she does display here some noble qualities even if they are directed towards an unworthy object in Merteuil. In addition, she takes her responsibility towards Cécile most solemnly, although once again she is sorely deceived about her true interest. If Mme de Volanges is duped and betrayed by her ostensible friends, she is herself not an evil individual, but rather a misguided one who tries her best to do what is right even when her best is far from sufficient.

And yet Mme de Volanges leaves the distinct impression of being a sinner as well as one sinned against. Such a strong negative judgment comes almost entirely from her presentation as a reader. Her most grievous fault is that she never listens to her daughter. The absence of any valid communication between mother and daughter is the most damning evidence we have against Mme de Volanges. Even if a written exchange would have been difficult to motivate or justify in terms of epistolary logic, the plain fact that they do not communicate in any fashion is indisputable since Cécile herself complains of not being able to talk with her mother. Not surprisingly, she quickly finds that Mme de Merteuil pays more attention to her than her own flesh and blood:

> C'est pourtant bien extraordinaire qu'une femme qui ne m'est presque pas parente, prenne plus de soin de moi que ma mère! (Letter 29, p. 61)

It is precisely this lack of a sympathetic listener or reader that defines the relationship between Cécile and Mme de Volanges. Indeed, all by itself, this noncommunication explains the inevitable tragedy that will send Cécile to a convent and leave her mother alone, shaken, and unable to fathom how and why this catastrophe took place.

Only on one occasion is Mme de Volanges her daughter's reader. Tipped off by the Marquise de Merteuil, she surprises Cécile in her room and confiscates her entire correspondence with Danceny, which up until then had been a well-kept secret. Mme de Volanges therefore becomes her daughter's reader only through force, and furthermore, through unlawful force since on this occasion her authority oversteps its bounds. Such use of force of course negates the true meaning of being a reader, which usually supposes a great deal of intimacy. There is no shared confidence, no mutual respect, no willing exchange of thoughts and feelings between them. It is ironic but entirely fitting in terms of the plot that Mme de Volanges be an intrusive, spying, and dishonest reader for her own daughter. The positive aspect of the readerly relationship which implies friendship, openness, and sharing is denied her. Cécile confides in the Marquise because she cannot speak to her own mother. In usurping Mme de Volanges's rightful place as confidante and confessor, even as mother, Merteuil perverts the true spirit of reading. But it is always Cécile who suffers, and doubly, from these two distortions of the reader's potential. Cécile's seduction and victimization by both Valmont and Merteuil derive ultimately from this same fact, namely that the normal and healthy relationship of confiding and exchanging, of having and of being a reader, was impossible for Mme de Volanges and her daughter. The maternal inability to act as a receiver and reader not only foreshadows the filial abandonment but actually causes it. As a failed reader, Mme de Volanges is responsible for her daughter's downfall; she causes Cécile's immoral conduct to the extent that she turned a deaf ear to her. Because she refuses to become her own daughter's confidante and friend, Mme de Volanges earns our negative assessment as insensitive, blind, and too wrapped up in herself. Had she been able to listen and to hear, she could have avoided for her own daughter the terrible fate that she sees so clearly as threatening the Présidente. In both of her letters to Mme de Tourvel, Mme de Volanges accurately identifies the danger that the Présidente is running:

> La seule chose que j'aie à vous dire, c'est que, de toutes les femmes auxquelles il [Valmont] a rendu des soins, succès ou non, il n'en est point qui n'aient eu à s'en plaindre. (Letter 9, p. 23)

Ironically for herself, she pleads with the Présidente to accept her warnings with the confidence and the sureness that characterize any true communication of mind and heart:

> Ah! revenez, revenez, je vous en conjure. Si mes raisons ne suffisent pas pour vous persuader, cédez à mon amitié; c'est elle qui me fait renouveller mes instances, c'est à elle à les justifier. (Letter 32, p. 66)

In all that concerns the Présidente, Mme de Volanges is attentive, her judgments are perceptive, and her warnings infallible, whereas she is totally mistaken about the dangers that threaten her own Cécile. For Mme de Tourvel, she remains a most perspicacious writer, while she can only be considered a criminally ineffectual reader for Cécile.

The Chevalier Danceny

The third personage who benefits from the distinction between writer and reader is the Chevalier Danceny. He is very much a fragmented figure who is only seen at certain points within the novel. He undergoes changes outside our view, beyond the ken of the fiction itself. In Danceny we see the product of a transformation rather than the process itself. An epistolary novel can reinforce the effect of such a disjointed characterization. By its very nature, the epistolary format is composed of discrete and discontinuous letters, of various narrators who take turns as the single voice and perspective through which the novel is presented, and of several plot lines followed simultaneously even when they do not intertwine. Thus the letter-novel is particularly well adapted to the type of sudden metamorphosis that Danceny experiences. The Chevalier can be successfully depicted as subject to these sudden modifications because he does not fix our attention with the same intensity as do main figures like Valmont, Merteuil, or Tourvel. He cannot support the same kind of close and relentless analysis as they do. Nonetheless, as a peripheral character, useful for reinforcing the symmetry of the seduction of the Présidente and Cécile, and as a foil for Valmont, Danceny profits from the distance that this discontinuous characterization allows. What interests us most here is that the Chevalier's fragmented character is revealed in several distinct stages not so much by what he himself says but rather by whom he listens to and reads. Danceny's discontinuous characterization is most effectively analyzed by reference to his role as a reader.

There are three distinct stages or periods of Danceny's personality. The first comprises his relationship to Cécile, and consequently his activity as writer and reader with her. In both functions, he is naive, unresourceful, and passive. He courts Mlle de Volanges by sending letters (in rather unusual if not entirely original fashion, it is true, by hiding them in her harp as mentioned in letter 16), but undertakes nothing more positive or daring until Valmont decides to assist him. As Cécile's reader, he is even more helpless. Each one of her letters to him provokes a different emotion. Several of Cécile's letters to her other correspondents contain a series of static views or snapshots of the Chevalier in his various moods and reactions. At first, only his pretty face and musical talent distinguish him from the rest of the crowd in the salon or drawing room:

> M. le chevalier Danceny, ce monsieur dont je t'ai parlé, et avec qui j'ai chanté chez Mme de Merteuil, a la complaisance de venir ici tous les jours, et de chanter avec moi des heures entières. Il est extrêmement aimable. Il chante comme un ange, et compose de très jolies airs dont il fait aussi les paroles. C'est bien dommage qu'il soit chevalier de Malte! (Letter 7, p. 20)

As he falls in love with Cécile, he displays the marks of an all-consuming passion, a romantic agony:

> Depuis il était devenu triste, mais si triste, si triste que ça me faisait de la peine; et quand je lui demandais pourquoi, il me disait que non; mais je voyais bien que si. Enfin hier il l'était encore plus que de coutume. (Letter 16, pp. 35-36)

When he does not receive a letter from Cécile, he is depressed:

> Je ne le regardai qu'un petit moment. Il ne me regardait pas, lui: mais il avait un air, qu'on aurait dit qu'il était malade.... Je rencontrai ses yeux, et il me fut impossible de détourner les miens. Un moment après je vis ses larmes couler. (Letter 18, p. 39)

But when he does receive one, his joy knows no bounds:

> Mais au retour, oh! comme il était content! En posant ma harpe vis-à-vis de moi, il se plaça de façon que Maman ne pouvait voir, et il prit ma main qu'il serra... mais d'une façon! (Letter 18, p. 40, ellipsis in original)

Despite his frequent outbursts of passionate words and expressions, Danceny seems incapable of realizing anything more audacious than holding hands. Never does he take any other liberties with Cécile. Only under Valmont's protection and guidance does he finally aspire to really enterprising behavior. When Mme de Volanges discovers his secret correspondence with Cécile, she firmly and irrevocably dismisses him from her salon. He does not dare to return.

During the second stage of his personal development, he is the Marquise de Merteuil's reader. Although there are but five letters corresponding to this period (three from Danceny, numbers 118, 148, and 150, and two from the Marquise, 121 and 146), this phase of Danceny's emotional and social evolution is a critical one. During this period he becomes more self-confident, more capable, more enterprising. In a word, the same Chevalier who was so ingenuous and respectful with Cécile has become a gallant companion and successful suitor of the Marquise. Since it is surely the Marquise who leads in this dance of mutual seduction, we can rightfully claim that Danceny, a nascent rake on the threshold of a libertine career of sexual triumphs, is indeed her product. He is learning from Merteuil's letters, just as Valmont once did, and he is being led by the nose just like Prévan, who suffered a resounding defeat at her hands. For Danceny to be the Marquise's reader implies equally that he is her pupil, her creature, and inevitably her victim: we have observed throughout this novel the wiles and skill of the Marquise enough not to doubt the outcome of this encounter. Whatever may be the eventual fate that Merteuil is preparing for him (but which never comes to fruition since the novel ends before that scheme matures), Danceny is a markedly different man when he reads the Marquise from the gauche young boy he was in his letters with Cécile. Mme de Merteuil herself points this out when remarking on the language that the Chevalier has just recently learned:

> Quittez donc, si vous m'en croyez, ce ton de cajolerie, qui n'est plus que du jargon, dès qu'il n'est pas l'expression de l'amour. Est-ce donc là le style de l'amitié? non, mon ami. (Letter 121, p. 283)

In any epistolary novel, characters are presented through the letters they write; they are created by their own words. Merteuil's comment is to be taken most seriously. The fact that his style has been corrupted by jargon is a critical and accurate reflection of his character.

Later, the Marquise invites him to pay her a secret visit on the eve of her departure from Paris, a visit that should remain secret even from Valmont whom Danceny still considers his true friend and confidant. Confidence is the ostensible topic of Merteuil's words, but her phrases betray a sentiment that is quite different as she attempts to provoke an entirely different kind of reaction in the Chevalier:

> Qui m'aurait dit, il y a quelque temps, que bientôt vous auriez ainsi ma confiance exclusive, je ne l'aurais pas cru. Mais la vôtre a entraîné la mienne. Je serais tentée de croire que vous y avez mis de l'adresse, peut-être même de la séduction. (Letter 146, pp. 341-42)

The Marquise is exaggerating Danceny's skill as a seducer, of course. Nevertheless, he does attempt to play this libertine role with her, even if she remains always in control of the situation and of her lover-pupil. This Chevalier talking love to the Marquise and initiating some sexual advances, even if she always calls the tune, is miles from the Danceny who could barely hold Cécile's hand.

The partial nature of Danceny's presentation and the unseen elements of his personal development (that is, unrecorded in the text that we are reading) are most apparent here. The progress of Merteuil and Danceny's relationship is clearly suggested, but even its main outlines are barely sketched. Moreover, we must beware the Marquise's own seductive technique. She is flattering Danceny and most probably giving him more credit than he deserves for winning and seducing her. Still, the end result is unmistakable. Danceny achieves with Mme de Merteuil the ultimate sexual communication which he could only dream of in his courtship of Cécile:

> O vous que j'aime! ô toi que j'adore! ô vous qui avez commencé mon bonheur! ô toi qui l'as comblé! Amie sensible, tendre amante. . . . Ainsi que moi, ma tendre amie, tu éprouvais, sans le connaître, ce charme impérieux qui livrait nos âmes aux douces impressions de la tendresse; et tous deux n'avons reconnu l'amour qu'en sortant de l'ivresse où ce dieu nous avait plongés. (Letter 148, pp. 346-47)

The rare use of the intimate *tu*-form suffices to explain the new relationship that now binds the Chevalier to the Marquise. It also emphasizes the raw power and the intensity of the emotion that Danceny is experiencing. Closing this hymn to their lovemaking, Danceny pretends to believe that he and Merteuil were inspired by their friendship alone and that they have not betrayed Cécile in giving expression to their passion:

> Hé! quels reproches avez-vous donc à vous faire? croyez-moi, votre délicatesse vous abuse. Les regrets qu'elle vous cause, les torts dont elle m'accuse, sont également illusoires. . . . Non, tu n'as pas trahi l'amitié, et je n'ai pas davantage abusé de ta confiance. (Letter 148, pp. 346-47)

Mme de Merteuil was not wrong, nor did she exaggerate in saying that Danceny had acquired a new language and all that new language implied. Danceny displays a total lack of moral principles to accompany his linguistic affectations. The jargon of the *petits maîtres* who seduced women with their deceptive words is rife in every one of his phrases and even more so in the obfuscating logic and tendentious rationale behind them.

Only because he enters into this epistolary contact with the Marquise de Merteuil does Danceny undergo this change in character. His transformation is due entirely to the Marquise. However, because a full presentation of this subplot is missing from the text, we have only a few traces of this period left in the five letters between Danceny and Merteuil. Rather than wishing there had been more development of this episode, we maintain that this partial presentation is sufficient as it stands. As brief as it is, it nonetheless suggests possible connections and symmetries with other actions in other plot lines of the novel. Most important, it is anchored in the concept of the reader. The reading connection between the Chevalier and the Marquise is indeed the only trace that even hints at Danceny's transformation. Merteuil's power over her reader is real, while Danceny's less active role as receiver of her message is underscored by his subordinate and even passive status as he is manipulated and seduced by her. Sexually and psychologically, Danceny exists in the shadow of Merteuil: the Marquise bends him to her will in terms both of personality and of text. For as long as he remains the Marquise de Merteuil's intended addressee (and we emphasize that term "intended" because it defines the precise nature of Merteuil's domination over Danceny while it also delimits the chronological duration of this relationship), he is also her plaything, her product, and her conquest.

The third and last of Danceny's faces derives once again from reading. His final experience as a reader in the novel changes him definitively. Afterwards, he recoils from the pretenses of society, he renounces the social whirl and all its attractions, and he flees Paris to embrace his once despised but original calling as a Knight of Malta. Reading Valmont's *cassette*, which contains his *Compte ouvert entre la marquise de Merteuil et le vicomte de Valmont*, is the event that provokes this drastic transformation. Now an avenger of iniquity and eager to compensate somehow for having killed Valmont in their duel, Danceny destroys the Marquise with the very papers and letters he has read. This third Danceny is markedly different from the other two personas and especially from the immediately preceding one. No longer Merteuil's intended reader, he escapes from her domination because she is not addressing him directly. In letters 121 and 146, she knew he was reading her and she wrote accordingly, with the intention of seducing him. Once he is no longer her intended reader, she loses her power over him.

Delivered after Valmont's death, these written revelations concerning Merteuil transform Danceny, their first outside reader, into a new man. Armed with this evidence which he owes to the reading half of his character, the Chevalier pursues the Marquise and avenges the Vicomte. Thanks to the knowledge he gains as a reader, as a writer he publishes Merteuil's own letter which details how she entrapped Prévan and exposed him to public ridicule and censure. Written in Merteuil's own hand, this letter is the Waterloo of that superb woman who compared herself to the Maréchal de Saxe as well as to God Himself. In his third and final incarnation, Danceny appears as an avenging angel who reestablishes the moral code and rights wrongs:

> J'ai cru, de plus, que c'était rendre un véritable service à la société que de démasquer une femme aussi réellement dangereuse que l'est Mme de Merteuil, et qui, comme vous pourrez le voir, est la seule, la véritable cause de tout ce qui s'est passé entre M. de Valmont et moi. (Letter 169, p. 382)

Thus, the reading process is itself critical in undoing Merteuil. More pointedly, we could say that Danceny destroys Merteuil because of what he has read as well as through what he has read. In a world of false appearances and deceptions of all sorts, reading alone can pass for an authentic activity which inspires confidence and guarantees veracity. By inviting Mme de Rosemonde to become, in her turn, another reader of Valmont's secret papers, Danceny shows to what extent he believes that the act of reading leads to the truth:

> N'en croyez pas mes discours; mais lisez, si vous en avez le courage, la correspondance que je dépose entre vos mains. (Letter 169, p. 382)

Danceny's belief in the positive power of the reading process transcends the limits of the novel itself. As the editors report in their footnote, the letters desposited by Danceny with Mme de Rosemonde will become the basis for the novel which they have edited and which we are reading. Laclos is cleverly prolonging his novel beyond its fictional space and into the real world that it mirrors. This is more than a simple game of illusions, however. Danceny's assurance that subsequent readers will react correctly, that is to say, that they will agree with him and approve his actions, is critical to the denouement of the novel and the punishment of the Marquise. Through Mme de Rosemonde, Danceny is reaching out to the other fictional readers, to all those in Merteuil's Paris, but also to the real reader in our world. More than any other character, Danceny is speaking out in the name of honesty and social morality in order to condemn vice and recommend virtue. He has not always been heard, since other times have found this novel either inaccurate in its depiction of society or immoral in its glorification of vice. Nonetheless, Danceny's injunction is to *read* and not to judge on any other criteria. A correct reading, we believe along with the Chevalier, would lead to an appropriately moral conclusion. But even more than that, Laclos is inviting us, through Danceny, to a literary event that precedes any consideration of morality: *lisez.*

Danceny's own story and the development of his personality can therefore best be understood as the result of his activity as a reader. Fresh, ineffectual, and unsure how to interpret the signs around him, he at first writes to Cécile and receives from her letters that are marked by their youth and inexperience. Reading the Marquise de Merteuil makes a different man out of him. He acquires a thin veneer of sophistication, joins the ranks of rakes and *petits maîtres,* and learns to speak a language debased by jargon. Reading Valmont posthumously transforms Danceny again. It gives him a mission to perform and opens new depths of knowledge both about himself and about the world surrounding him.

Mme de Rosemonde

Although we have already discussed Mme de Rosemonde both as the last fictional reader inside the novel and as the first real reader outside it, she can bear further comment here as we separate her character as addresser from that as addressee.

Whenever she writes letters, Mme de Rosemonde seems to be singularly misinformed about the true nature of her nephew. Perhaps she is simply blind to his shortcomings, perhaps she has decided not to recognize him for the rogue that he is. Her early letters to Mme de Tourvel are full of his praises even though she is forced on occasion to admit his all too obvious faults. Her loving interest in Valmont is combined with an almost comic inability to discover what is really happening and what the Vicomte is actually doing. For example, she completely misinterprets Valmont's shock and disappointment at the Présidente's early morning departure from the château as the effects of a mild cold:

> Mon neveu est aussi un peu indisposé, mais sans aucun danger, et sans qu'il faille en prendre aucune inquiétude; c'est une incommodité légère, qui, à ce qu'il me semble, affecte plus son humeur que sa santé. Nous ne le voyons presque plus. (Letter 112, p. 263)

She also misconstrues Cécile's tiredness, and fails even to suspect those nocturnal meetings which have caused such obvious fatigue:

> La petite Volanges, surtout, vous trouve furieusement à dire, et bâille, tant que la journée dure, à avaler ses poings. (Letter 112, p. 263)

We can smile at Mme de Rosemonde's observation since we know that Valmont and Cécile are spending their nights in bed together, he giving a course in libertinage, she becoming a star pupil.

By the end of the novel, her opinion has not changed substantially. Even though she has learned all the details of the Vicomte's seduction and betrayal of both the Présidente and Cécile, and of his ongoing libertine pact with the Marquise de Merteuil, she cannot bring herself to judge him harshly. In fact, she appears to blame only the Marquise for their joint conduct:

> Après ce que vous m'avez fait connaître, Monsieur [Danceny], il ne reste qu'à pleurer et se taire. On regrette de vivre encore, quand on apprend de pareilles horreurs; on rougit d'être femme, quand on en voit une capable de semblables excès. (Letter 171, p. 386)

She is honest enough, however, to recognize her weakness for her nephew and her unshakable attachment to him:

> Malgré ses torts, que je suis forcée de reconnaître, je sens que je ne me consolerai jamais de sa perte. (Letter 171, p. 386)

"Forced to recognize" his wrongs is not an exaggeration. Until she received Danceny's unimpeachable evidence against the Vicomte, Mme de Rosemonde was prepared to go to the limit of the law in favor of her nephew:

> mon intention est que vous en rendiez plainte sur-le-champ, et en mon nom. En pardonnant à son ennemi, à son meurtrier, mon neveu a pu satisfaire à sa générosité naturelle; mais moi, je dois venger à la fois sa mort, l'humanité et la religion. (Letter 164, p. 373)

Even though she is aware of the Présidente's ordeal at Valmont's hands, Mme de Rosemonde can without sarcasm or irony still speak of his "generosity" (which doubtless retains part of its etymological sense of one who acts nobly so as to win honor for himself and his family), accuse Danceny of being a murderer (both adversaries were willing and fairly matched even if dueling was illegal), and invoke principles like humanity and religion even though in his life Valmont respected neither.

However commendable Mme de Rosemonde's attachment to the Vicomte might be under normal circumstances, it certainly does not do justice to his many victims nor can it claim any logical or justifiable origin in his own conduct and attitude towards others. On this score Mme de Rosemonde disappoints us, since she chooses to ignore the question of whether Valmont really deserves her uncritical affection.

As a reader, however, Mme de Rosemonde is quite different from what she is as a narrator and as a third party described by other correspondents. As a reader, she is particularly aware of Valmont's faults and remains acutely attentive to the best ways of resisting him and his charms. The letters which Mme de Tourvel addresses to her, especially after the Présidente's flight from the château to Paris, document the Vicomte's unconscionable behavior as well as the terrible dilemma that loving him poses for the Présidente. It is remarkable that, given her usual defensive and protective attitude about Valmont, Mme de Rosemonde listens so sympathetically to all that the Présidente reports about the moral difficulties that Valmont's aggressive conduct has caused. Then she encourages the Présidente to confide in her even more! As a writer she may be Valmont's aunt, but as a reader, she becomes Mme de Tourvel's mother:

> Regardez-moi comme votre enfant. Ayez pour moi les bontés maternelles; je les implore. . . . O vous, que je choisis pour ma mère, recevez-en le serment. (Letter 102, pp. 235-36)

In the world of the *Liaisons dangereuses,* however, a mother is neither a powerful nor an efficacious figure. Mme de Volanges was incapable of protecting her daughter, and Mme de Rosemonde is guarded in estimating the value of the succor she can offer to the Présidente:

> En laissant à la Providence le soin de vous secourir dans un danger contre lequel je ne peux rien, je me réserve de vous soutenir et vous consoler autant qu'il sera en moi. (Letter 103, p. 238)

Unable either to save the Présidente or to stop loving her nephew, powerless to act as a protective mother or a disciplining aunt, Mme de Rosemonde is split by her affections and the two distinct mental states they imply. Like the other personages examined in this chapter, her double character is best illustrated by separating the two strands of her fictional nature and by studying her both as a writer and as a reader.

5

Writer vs. Reader: The Struggle for Power

In addition to the interpersonal conflicts that result in the seduction of Mme de Tourvel and the corruption of Cécile Volanges, the mockery made of Danceny, and the revenge exacted against both the Comte de Gercourt and Mme de Volanges, another, more important struggle takes place throughout this entire novel. At the very center of the *Liaisons dangereuses*, Mme de Merteuil and the Vicomte de Valmont vie with each other to see which of them will be the most libertine, the most corrupt, and the most corrupting.

Before the novel began, the Marquise and the Vicomte had been lovers. Some residue of this original affection surely remains, since they still are friends and write to each other frequently and confidentially. They even allude to the possibility of once again becoming lovers. Valmont plans to dispose of the Présidente quickly so as to return to Paris and collect his reward from the Marquise:

> Cela me fait songer que vous m'avez promis une infidélité en ma faveur; j'en ai votre promesse par écrit. (Letter 57, p. 117)

For her part, the Marquise encourages Valmont to return to her arms, but only after he has seduced la Présidente and only if he brings with him proof of his victory and Mme de Tourvel's defeat:

> Aussitôt que vous aurez eu votre belle dévote, que vous pourrez m'en fournir une preuve, venez, et je suis à vous. Mais vous n'ignorez pas que dans les affaires importantes, on ne reçoit de preuves que par écrit. Par cet arrangement, d'une part, je deviendrai une récompense au lieu d'être une consolation. (Letter 20, p. 42)

Despite their continued and mutual epistolary confidences and this promise of imminent reconciliation crowned by the physical act of love, and despite even the real possibility that the Marquise loves Valmont deeply and acts against him only out of motives of jealousy and spite, Merteuil and Valmont are in fact bitter enemies and deadly rivals. The intense competition between them as well as their own towering pride leads directly to their downfall. Each one is more than capable of destroying the other, and each one succeeds in doing precisely that. Just as the strategies by which they acquire power differ, so their ways of using that power vary. Now I propose to examine their long journey from love to hate from the perspective of writer and reader and to see how these twin narrative functions articulate this battle of the sexes. Once the various libertine projects in the plot are exhausted, this monumental power struggle becomes an infrastructural contest, pitting the masculine, offensive, and attacking strategy of an excellent narrator against the feminine, counterattacking, and more defensive techniques of a highly aware and skillful reader.

The Written Battle Lines

Merteuil and Valmont are most conscious of their status as members of an exclusive elite, both social and intellectual. That this elite represents the triumph of evil over good is of no importance to them. They both aspire to the highest realms of their chosen careers even though their activities rank very low on any scale of moral values. Both are supremely confident of their inborn superiority. In Valmont's words:

> En vérité, plus je vais, et plus je suis tenté de croire qu'il n'y a que vous et moi dans le monde, qui valions quelque chose. (Letter 100, p. 232)

Consequently, they are never modest in choosing comparisons for themselves. The Marquise likens herself to the great general, the Maréchal de Saxe (letter 63, p. 124), while the Vicomte sees himself as Turenne, Frédéric de Prusse, and Hannibal (letter 125, p. 298), and in another place as Alexander the Great:

> je ne vois alors dans vos amants que les successeurs d'Alexandre, incapables de conserver entre eux tous cet empire où je régnais seul. (Letter 15, p. 34)

These military comparisons express accurately Valmont and Merteuil's consciousness of their own superiority. Not illogically then, their power struggle acquires all the trappings of a full-fledged armed conflict. As the moment of their definitive and irrevocable falling-out approaches, Valmont sends the Marquise a letter whose tone leaves no doubt about the intensity of his emotions:

> J'attends votre réponse. Songez en la faisant, songez bien que plus il vous est facile encore de me faire oublier l'offense que vous m'avez faite, plus un refus de votre part, un simple délai, la graverait dans mon cœur en traits ineffaçables. (Letter 151, p. 354)

In a subsequent letter he promises to be either her lover or her enemy:

> de ce jour même je serai votre amant, ou votre ennemi. (Letter 153, p. 357)

Merteuil's response is brief but telling, since it continues the military imagery: "Hé bien! la guerre" (letter 153, p. 358). Underneath the thin skin of these decorous letters and of the ultracivilized persons writing and receiving them beat ferocious and warlike hearts that do not recoil from even the most murderous gestures. After having lured Valmont into betraying the Présidente, whom she suspects he really does love and therefore prefers to herself, Mme de Merteuil exults that she has both eliminated a dangerous rival and demonstrated her superiority over the Vicomte:

> C'est dommage qu'avec tant de talent pour les projets, vous en ayez si peu pour l'exécution; et que par une seule démarche inconsidérée, vous ayez mis vous-même un obstacle invincible à ce que vous désirez le plus. (Letter 145, p. 340)

Merteuil's hatred for Mme de Tourvel is intense. However, the jealousy and rage behind her brutal attack against the Présidente should not divert our attention from another motive and from another military objective. By eliminating the Présidente as a rival for Valmont's love, she is striking at Valmont himself and defeating him. She has caused him to bend his will to hers: he has given up Mme de Tourvel, whom he loves, upon the order of the Marquise. This episode illustrates, just as the extensive use of the military metaphor does, that the libertine code is not merely one of sexual gratification. More important, it is also an effort to dominate and to control others, to overpower their will, and to possess them spiritually as well as sexually.

A further indication of Valmont and Merteuil's conviction that they are superior beings who belong almost to another world is once again linguistic. In addition to military metaphors, they employ a figurative language that is heavily loaded with religious terms. As they describe their immoral projects in sacred terms, Merteuil and Valmont blaspheme knowingly and willingly. Under the Vicomte's pen we find on numerous occasions expressions like *ange, adorable, dévote, céleste,* and *divine,* to describe Mme de Tourvel. In his very first presentation of the Présidente, Valmont introduces this religious element. He joins Mmes de Tourvel and de Rosemonde in their "prières du matin et du soir" and "pieux entretiens." His aunt is far from suspecting his true purposes and intentions:

> elle est édifiée de me voir régulièrement à ses prières et à sa messe. Elle ne se doute pas de la divinité que j'y adore. (Letter 4, p. 14)

To culminate his seduction Valmont has recourse to a priest, the Père Anselme, who unknowingly arranges that final meeting during which the Présidente succumbs to her seducer. The Vicomte's blasphemous use of figurative language, which marks his relationship to Mme de Tourvel so distinctly, extends then even to the characters associated with her. This linguistic sin distorts and destroys the personal, confidential bonds that should characterize love as well as the social and contractual links of marriage. One libertine project easily encompasses the reversal of many other religious, social, and personal values.

Valmont is, of course, not the only one who indulges in such blasphemous behavior. Mme de Merteuil abrogates to herself almost divine powers.

> Me voilà comme la Divinité, recevant les vœux opposés des aveugles mortels, et ne changeant rien à mes décrets immuables. (Letter 63, p. 126)

In her account of her formative years and her self-education as a liberated woman and a libertine, she claims to have created herself. Like God, she is her own cause and her own product: "et je puis dire que je suis mon ouvrage" (letter 81, p. 175). After years of perfecting "ce travail sur moi-même" which separates her from other women and which elevates her above even the men of her times ("ces tyrans détrônés devenus mes esclaves"), the Marquise reaches her present point of perfection, described with a biblical example:

> Nouvelle Dalila, j'ai toujours, comme elle, employé ma puissance à surprendre ce secret important. De combien de nos Samsons modernes, ne tiens-je pas la chevelure sous le ciseau! (Letter 81, p. 179)

It is not at all surprising that words like "diabolical" and "satanic" have come to mind for critics who want to capture the extreme nature of Merteuil's personality. She does bring the most accomplished and formidable skills to her licentious projects. Like Lucifer, another brilliant individual who refused to serve for the good, the Marquise has chosen to place her talents and her intelligence in the service of evil.

Immoral plans, seductions, corruptions, and vengeances directed against others cannot in the end however satisfy the need that both Valmont and Merteuil feel to prove themselves. Their enemies are too weak, their targets too easy. The victims they attack, like Mme de Tourvel or Cécile, are helpless since they do not understand the libertine's conduct or his principles. Because they do not comprehend the nature of the attack directed against them, they do not know how best to resist it. In the face of such undemanding challenges there is only one alternative. The ultimate test for elite seducers like the Marquise and the Vicomte is to take on each other. It is not at all unworthy of this libertine context that, in this central conflict between the main protagonists, love becomes hate, friendship is transformed into rivalry, and confidence and affection are transmuted into depersonalization and contempt. Perhaps the most libertine act and the most corrupting gesture of this entire novel is that Valmont and Merteuil consciously and willingly allow their love to be betrayed into hatred.

Only Valmont can provide a worthy adversary for Merteuil, just as she alone knows how to offer an effective defense against his sexual advances. In the end, their own pride demands such a confrontation and leads them into a tragic and fatal conflict. An overwhelming desire to be recognized as superior by an adversary of their own caliber and in a combat whose true nature and rules are known to both combatants forces them into a definitive struggle which will determine who is first and foremost. The prize cannot be shared, there is no room for two champion libertines. It must be one or the other, since each feels that same imperious and exclusive need to be acknowledged superior by the other.

In that autobiographical letter 81 in which she describes her godlike self-creation, Mme de Merteuil proclaims directly and brutally that she is better than Valmont:

> Que vos craintes me causent de pitié! Combien elles me prouvent ma supériorité sur vous! et vous voulez m'enseigner, me conduire! Ah! mon pauvre Valmont, quelle distance il y a encore de vous à moi! (Letter 81, p. 172)

Her immoral projects are not only more difficult than his, but he would also be incapable of performing them: "Parce que vous ne pourriez exécuter mes projets, vous les jugez impossibles!" (letter 81, p. 172). Her confidence in her own superior ability crushes his unjustified pride, a typically unfounded male pride that, according to her, is nothing but self-delusion:

> Non, tout l'orgueil de votre sexe ne suffirait pas pour remplir l'intervalle qui nous sépare. (Letter 81, p. 172)

The Marquise's unshakable certitude about her superiority over Valmont finds full expression in phrases which translate her scorn for his amatory successes and her deprecation of his minimal worth in the face of her outstanding achievements:

> Et qu'avez-vous donc fait, que je n'aie surpassé mille fois? (Letter 81, p. 172)

In an equally revealing comment, Merteuil discloses just how much her original affection for Valmont was inspired by an emotion not far from the deadly rivalry we are now discussing. The love Merteuil had for the Vicomte is perhaps but a form of self-love:

> je vous désirais avant de vous avoir vu. Séduite par votre réputation, il me semblait que vous manquiez à ma gloire; je brûlais de vous combattre corps à corps. (Letter 81, p. 180)

The fully charged sexuality of terms like *je brûlais* and *corps à corps* cannot hide her profoundly antagonist feelings which are betrayed by other key words like *ma gloire* and *vous combattre*. The Marquise has a well-founded belief in her own formidable talents:

> Si pourtant vous m'avez vue, disposant des événements et des opinions, faire de ces hommes si redoutables les jouets de mes caprices ou de mes fantaisies. . . . (Letter 81, p. 174)

Such confidence permits her to distinguish herself from all other women whose defeat is always imminent:

> imprudentes, qui dans leur amant actuel ne savent pas voir leur ennemi futur! (Letter 81, p. 174)

Merteuil's criticism of those who are not prepared to recognize how love and rivalry mix warns us not to make that same mistake with her. She never forgets that although Valmont had been her past lover, he will also certainly become her future adversary.

Merteuil comes close to denouncing the entire male sex as her enemy. Her strident complaint against all men is rather the direct outgrowth of her private quarrel with just one man. For the Marquise's denunciation of what she sees as woman's unjustifiably inferior condition in relation to man springs from her own private dispute as an individual against the man whom she accuses of being ranked above her while possessing less talent and merit than she does.

Despite harsh exchanges like these, Valmont and Merteuil continue to write each other and to remain, at least for the first two-thirds of the novel, friends and confidants. To her, he reports his slow progress in seducing the Présidente as well as the undefinable pleasure he finds in the latter's virtuous resistance:

> Ah! qu'elle se rende, mais qu'elle combatte; que, sans avoir la force de vaincre, elle ait celle de résister; qu'elle savoure à loisir le sentiment de sa faiblesse, et soit contrainte d'avouer sa défaite. . . . Ce projet est sublime, n'est-ce pas? (Letter 23, p. 50)

The small details of this courtship and the little victories along the way enchant the Vicomte:

> et à la porte de son appartement elle a serré la mienne [sa main] avec force. Il est vrai que ce mouvement m'a paru avoir quelque chose d'involontaire: mais tant mieux; c'est une preuve de plus de mon empire. (Letter 99, p. 228)

The Marquise interprets all this quite differently. She denigrates Valmont's skill, his intelligence, and his value as a rake. When Mme de Tourvel flees both the château and the Vicomte, who thought himself on the eve of total victory, Merteuil gloats over his failure:

> Vous voilà donc absolument réduit à rien! et cela entre deux femmes [i.e., Tourvel and Cécile], dont l'une était déjà au lendemain, et l'autre ne demandait pas mieux que d'y être! (Letter 106, p. 248)

How does she explain Valmont's inability to defeat the Présidente and his recent misunderstandings with Cécile, whom she, the Marquise, had carefully prepared for him to debauch? She suggests again his marked inferiority by an implicit comparison with her own talents of invention and imagination:

> C'est que réellement vous n'avez pas le génie de votre état; vous n'en savez que ce que vous en avez appris, et vous n'inventez rien. (Letter 106, p. 248)

Merteuil is therefore, at least in her own opinion, the superior libertine because she creates new strategems and tricks, while Valmont can only copy and repeat. Consequently his reputation as a rogue and rake is overvalued. The Marquise would like to see him more accurately assessed, which would mean at a value obviously inferior to her own:

> Enfin, il faut vous attendre à être apprécié peut-être autant au-dessous de votre valeur, que vous l'avez été au-dessus jusqu'à présent. (Letter 113, p. 264)

Throughout this one-upmanship contest both the Vicomte and the Marquise are fully conscious of the mortal danger they are running. Valmont neatly sums up their situation of mutual destructive power:

> De longs discours n'étaient pas nécessaires pour établir que chacun de nous ayant en main tout ce qu'il faut pour perdre l'autre, nous avons un égal intérêt à nous ménager mutuellement. (Letter 153, p. 357)

On her side Merteuil recognizes the same vulnerability because she has confided in Valmont just as he has confessed his intimate thoughts to her:

> A la vérité, je vous ai depuis livré tous mes secrets. (Letter 81, p. 180)

Yet each one's desire to be recognized as the best risks undoing the confidential exchanges and the bonds of mutual respect and assistance that had previously united them and made their libertine intrigues successful. Now, as their overweening pride and absolute need to dominate lead them down separate paths, they are losing whatever understanding and intimate communication once linked them together, not to mention their past love, whose memory lingers but which is fading into the past:

> C'est une chose inconcevable, ma belle amie, comme aussitôt qu'on s'éloigne, on cesse facilement de s'entendre. Tant que j'étais auprès de vous, nous n'avions jamais qu'un même sentiment; . . . depuis près de trois mois, je ne vous vois plus, nous ne sommes plus de même avis sur rien. (Letter 115, p. 271)

The bond that unites them is fragile indeed: three months' absence suffices to undo years of confidential communications. In a self-referential sense, the epistolary novel itself forces this rupture. Writing letters, without which the novel could not exist in its present form, is motivated only by physical absence. The very fact of writing is already an indication of the inevitable break-up. The catastrophe of the denouement is imbedded, as in tragedy, in the very premises that permit its origin. This story of seductions realized by the Valmont-Merteuil pair takes place in and through letters. At the same time, the dissolution of that same libertine couple occurs because of these very same letters. The letters that seduce the Présidente also destroy Valmont's confidential relationship with the Marquise. Writing and receiving letters is therefore a double-edged sword whose undermining and corrupting properties are radical. In the end, the same letters will ruin both the innocent and the guilty. For the moment, however, we have not yet arrived at that point of complete misunderstanding and open hostilities between Valmont and Merteuil.

That verb *s'entendre,* quoted above, contains a powerful litotes. For the Vicomte and the Marquise, "understanding" encompasses the love that dates back to before the beginning of the novel; the mutual confidence, secrets, and correspondences they have shared; and the support, recognition, and validation they have provided for each other. Since both of them are so powerful, closely matched in guile and ruthlessness, Valmont is merely repeating the obvious when he says that they should treat each other carefully: "nous ménager mutuellement" (letter 153, p. 357). They should. But they do not. Each is too proud, too haughty, to accept second best. Going one step further, we could even say that each one is offended deeply and personally by the very presence and more so by the success of the other. They both brag and exalt themselves in these letters, which, as they rub such highly sensitive and much distended egos in precisely the wrong way, are metamorphosed from tokens of love and confidence into the actual weapons of rivalry and combat.

Once this war of pride is declared ("Hé bien! la guerre," in the words of the Marquise in letter 153), it can only be a struggle to the death. The prize that is being contested as well as the self-image that each combatant has placed squarely on the line assures us that no compromise is possible and that no quarter will be asked or given.

> Non, quoi que vous en disiez, c'est un retour impossible. D'abord, j'exigerais des sacrifices que sûrement vous ne pourriez ou ne voudriez pas faire, et qu'il se peut bien que je ne mérite pas; et puis, comment vous fixer? Oh! non, non. (Letter 131, p. 312)

The Marquise's semi-sweet recollections of their past happiness do not change her awareness that they have no future together. Their egos and interests are now too far apart. The only alternative is to back off, to divide the spoils, and to leave the field of battle, a possibility that the Marquise suggests in a little anecdote:

> Vous savez l'histoire de ces deux fripons, qui se reconnurent en jouant: nous ne nous ferons rien, se dirent-ils, payons les cartes par moitié; et ils quittèrent la partie. Suivons, croyez-moi, ce prudent exemple.... (Letter 131, p. 311)

If they do not split their winnings and call it quits, a catastrophic falling-out is inevitable: "Mais, dites-moi, Vicomte, qui de nous deux se chargera de tromper l'autre?" (letter 131, p. 311).

The Readerly Armageddon

Valmont and Merteuil adopt very different styles of fighting in their last and culminating confrontation. The reader and his or her power will determine the winning tactics and provide the decisive weapons in this licentious Armageddon. We have already seen Valmont oppose his male *autorité* to the Marquise's feminine *finesse*. In her turn, Merteuil offers her own view of their differing strategies, opposing the male offense to feminine defense:

> Supposons, j'y consens, que vous mettiez autant d'adresse à nous vaincre que nous à nous défendre ou à céder. (Letter 81, p. 173)

However, she implies the superiority of women, first by that sarcastic concession (*supposons*), and second by suggesting that the woman is victorious or at least the equal of the man either when she gives in or refuses. Indeed, as these differing formulations suggest, Valmont and Merteuil have each displayed a continuous preference for a single strategy throughout the novel, which we can see in their contacts and conflicts with other characters. Valmont is an active and aggressive seducer. He attacks the Présidente frontally just as he adopts a direct offensive against Cécile. This aggressive strategy coincides neatly with his status as the principal narrator of the novel. To a large extent his seductive offensives depend on his being a narrator and thus controlling the writing function which naturally initiates action in an epistolary novel.

Mme de Merteuil, on the other hand, prefers a defensive tactic. She appears passive, possibly helpless, in this war between the sexes. This is, of course, the traditional woman's role: a citadel besieged and invested until the conquering hero takes possession of that seat of resistance.[1] Profiting from the very nature of this defensive strategy, the Marquise has become a master of the counterattack, the surprise maneuver, and the quickly sprung trap, as Prévan learned to his astonishment and dismay. While she is an expert narrator, the Marquise's principal strength lies in her ability to exploit her function as a reader. In contrast to the active and initiating narrator, the more passive reader plays a waiting game, observing and absorbing whatever gambits the writer offers. The struggle between Merteuil and Valmont becomes then a classic confrontation of two evenly matched but tactically contrasting opponents. We can amplify this opposition by a number of symmetries: man vs. woman; the obviously strong vs. the apparently weak; attacker vs. defender; frontal assault vs. surprise ambush; strength vs. finesse; and in terms most relevant to our concern with narrative technique, the writer vs. the reader; the sender vs. the receiver; and the addresser vs. the addressee.

We have already made the distinction between Valmont, illegal reader and thief, and Merteuil, invited listener and secret reader. We have seen how both of them use their status as a reader in their seductions of other characters. Now we will focus on the single role, writer or reader, that best characterizes each one in their direct confrontation.

In their reciprocal correspondence, Valmont characteristically plays the initiator and narrator, writing thirty-four letters to the Marquise, while she occupies the receiving position, as reader, writing to him only twenty-one times. However, this distinction is somewhat paradoxical since what the Marquise loses because she writes less, she gains since she reads more. These figures (thirty-four vs. twenty-one letters written) and the proportions they represent (Valmont writes half again as many as Merteuil) would be of little interest if we did not explore the benefits that the Marquise derives from being the apparently weaker figure, the passive and defensive reader. The dynamics of this exchange between writer and reader articulate the libertine struggle to dominate the other.

Of primary importance is the fact that Mme de Merteuil is Valmont's secret and supplementary reader in that she reads the letters he addresses to Mme de Tourvel. She is an intrusive reader, admitted as an unseen third party into the private exchange between the Vicomte and the Présidente, spying on them both and yet hidden from the original addressee. Letters 47 and 48 are sent to the Marquise, who reads both of them (that is, Valmont's duplicitous protestations of love and his libertine gloss of it) and who then forwards the second one to the Présidente, to whom it is addressed. In reading both these letters which Laclos has intentionally juxtaposed, we as readers of the entire novel undergo a direct experience of Valmont's duplicity. From the shocking contrast of the content of these two letters, augmented by the fillip of their close proximity, we judge Valmont and his character. Similarly, the Marquise, who enjoys through her own reading a perspective much like our own, wins an advantage over the Vicomte. Every time that Valmont voluntarily submits to Merteuil those letters he has written to and for the Présidente, he is conceding an important tactical weapon to her. Without fully realizing the damage he is inflicting upon himself, Valmont is stocking Merteuil's arsenal with facts and information that she uses most effectively in the continuous competition and in the ongoing criticisms that prelude their final, deadly combat. From Valmont's own mouth, as it were, she obtains an inside look at his successes and failures. So armed, her criticisms of his seduction of Mme de Tourvel are devastatingly accurate. She sums up in pithy fashion Valmont's obvious pleasure in prolonging his contact with Mme de Tourvel even when it is at the expense of completing his seduction of her:

> vous désirez moins de vaincre que de combattre. (Letter 33, p. 66)

She can follow his attack from a safe distance, but still close enough to observe the ebb and flow of the battle, especially when it turns to the Vicomte's disadvantage:

> Aussi, malgré l'avantage que vous aviez pris sur elle dans votre conversation, elle vous bat dans sa lettre.... Savez-vous que cette femme a plus de force que je ne croyais? sa défense est bonne. (Letter 33, pp. 67, 68)

If the Présidente's defense is good, then the Vicomte's attack is at fault. The corollary is implicit in this cleverly backhanded compliment. The stinging reproach to Valmont's pride is no less strong for being hidden. Once again, in the seduction of Cécile, the Marquise enjoys a double perspective over Valmont's correspondence and consequently over his activities. Once more not only is she able to criticize what Valmont fails to accomplish, but she can also denigrate what he succeeds in doing:

> Vous l'avez trouvée [Cécile] sous la main, vous l'avez prise: à la bonne heure! mais ce ne peut pas être là un goût. Ce n'est pas même, à vrai dire, une entière jouissance: vous ne possédez absolument que son corps! je ne parle pas de son cœur, dont je me doute bien que vous ne vous souciez guère: mais vous n'occupez seulement pas sa tête. (Letter 113, p. 267)

When Mme de Tourvel, hopelessly in love with the Vicomte but still unwilling to admit it, leaves the château and flees to Paris, Valmont writes these desperate lines to the Marquise:

> Mon amie, je suis joué, trahi, perdu; je suis au désespoir: Mme de Tourvel est partie. Elle est partie, et je ne l'ai pas su! (Letter 100, p. 229)

His previous letter (99) had predicted the Présidente's imminent surrender:

> il est vrai que je compte demain, puisqu'elle [his victory over the Présidente] ne sera véritablement consommée qu'alors. (Letter 99, p. 229)

Proud and victorious one day, defeated and outraged the next, Valmont hides nothing of his private emotional life from Mme de Merteuil, who is his intimate and confidential reader. She receives all this information directly from him and stocks it away for eventual use against him. Thanks to these confessions, she can be condescending and speak of her affection for him because, as she contemplates his setbacks and enjoys his discomfort, she fears him less as a rival:

> A merveille, vicomte, et pour le coup, je vous aime à la fureur! Au reste, après la première de vos deux lettres [number 99], on pouvait s'attendre à la seconde [100]; aussi ne m'a-t-elle point étonnée. (Letter 106, p. 247)

Strong in her newfound sense of superiority, the Marquise can proceed to criticize Valmont's attack, to point out his mistakes, and thereby to relegate him to the second rank of libertines, well behind herself:

> Que voulez-vous que fasse une pauvre femme qui se rend, et qu'on ne prend pas? . . . Vous voilà donc absolument réduit à rien! . . . vous allez croire que je me vante, et dire qu'il est facile de prophétiser après l'événement: mais je peux vous jurer que je m'y attendais. (Letter 106, pp. 247-48)

Mme de Merteuil proclaims Valmont's inferiority and her own superiority based on the information that he himself has been foolish enough to supply. In his overly aggressive eagerness to attack and seduce, as well as in his desire to narrate these victories even before they are won (and we note here in passing the coincidence of the narrating and the libertine projects), Valmont as writer falls into the trap prepared for him by the Marquise as reader. She can comment upon his tactical mistakes and his unsuccessful initiatives only because he provides the ammunition that she turns against him.

For his own part, the Vicomte never achieves this kind of victory over Mme de Merteuil. When Valmont becomes a secret, supplementary reader, it is usually by theft or force, tactics that are much less effective that Merteuil's ability to secure the cooperation and the complicity of the narrator in his own self-incrimination. Moreover, those occasions when the Vicomte does acquire power as an extra or remote reader involve the Présidente or Cécile.

Mme de Merteuil remains untouched by Valmont's successes as a hidden reader.

Of course, Valmont is the Marquise's addressee and intended reader on those twenty-one occasions when she writes directly to him. Does he draw any advantage from his position as a reader of her letters which might be comparable to what she learns as a reader of his? Quite simply, no, as a brief comparison of Merteuil's retelling of the Prévan episode with Valmont's account of his seduction of the Présidente clearly reveals.

Because she is a hidden reader, intruding into Valmont's letters to Mme de Tourvel, as well as his ongoing confidante and intended addressee in the day-by-day struggle to seduce the latter, the Marquise de Merteuil observes Valmont at close range and notices all the errors in his libertine campaign. Valmont can hide neither his plans (tomorrow the Présidente will succumb) nor his disappointments (she has left during the night). In marked contrast is Merteuil's account of her seduction of Prévan. When she writes her version, the battle is already over and her victory secure. Hence she risks absolutely nothing (at least, at first glance) by becoming a narrator and allowing Valmont to be her reader. She describes all the aspects of the episode as she pleases without fear that the facts might change and belie her neat final version of them. Merteuil is fully aware of the strategic edge she has here. She emphasizes that, as narrator, she deals only in definitive texts, while in parallel fashion, as a libertine, she prefers open and shut affairs:

> J'ai mis à fin mon aventure avec Prévan; à fin! entendez-vous bien ce que cela veut dire? (Letter 85, p. 188)

What this really means is that although Valmont does read this potentially dangerous account written by Merteuil herself, he obtains no advantage from it, he learns nothing to turn against her, he fails to acquire thereby any power over her. By offering only this fixed and unchangeable version to Valmont, Merteuil has emptied the function of reader of its value as observer and confidant, a value that she nonetheless continues to exploit fully in her own eavesdropping on the Valmont-Tourvel exchange. Her presentation of the Prévan episode, both as a narrator's effort to thwart her reader of the power that naturally resides in the act of reading and as a libertine project of deception and humiliation, is a brilliant defensive maneuver since it denies Valmont any information or advantage even remotely comparable to what the Marquise obtains by being his reader.

The most instructive phase of the Valmont-Merteuil power struggle, at least as far as the opposition of reader and writer is concerned, takes place in the closing pages of the novel, after the seductions of Cécile and Mme de Tourvel have been completed. Once these libertine projects have been liquidated,

Merteuil and Valmont have nothing left to hide behind. What had served as pretext for criticisms, exercises in one-upmanship, and pretensions of superiority has finally disappeared. Now Valmont and Merteuil confront each other directly. The major battle, which inspired all the other skirmishes, is about to begin in earnest.

With words that underline his libertine motivations, Valmont exults in his victory over Mme de Tourvel:

> La voilà donc vaincue, cette femme superbe qui avait osé croire qu'elle pourrait me résister! (Letter 125, p. 292)

In the very same letter he describes in minute detail the scene of the Présidente succumbing to his advances:

> j'examinais soigneusement le local; et dès lors, je marquai de l'œil le théâtre de ma victoire. . . . dans cette même chambre, il se trouvait une ottomane. . . . Tandis que je parlais ainsi, je sentais son cœur palpiter avec violence; j'observais l'altération de sa figure; je voyais surtout les larmes la suffoquer. . . . A ce dernier mot elle se précipita, ou plutôt tomba évanouie entre mes bras . . . je la conduisais, ou la portais, vers le lieu précédemment désigné pour le champ de ma gloire; et en effet, elle ne revint à elle que soumise et déjà livrée à son heureux vainqueur. . . . Ce fut avec cette candeur naïve ou sublime qu'elle me livra sa personne et ses charmes et qu'elle augmenta mon bonheur en le partageant. L'ivresse fut complète et réciproque; et pour la première fois, la mienne survécut au plaisir. (Letter 125, pp. 294; 298-300)

Having finally completed the seduction of Mme de Tourvel, Valmont claims to have fulfilled his part of the bargain struck with the Marquise early in the novel:

> Vous voyez que je m'exécute, et que, comme je vous l'ai promis, mes affaires seront assez avancées pour que je puisse vous donner une partie de mon temps. (Letter 125, p. 300)

He demands that she do her part:

> Dépêchez-vous donc de renvoyer votre pesant Belleroche, et laissez-là le doucereux Danceny, pour ne vous occuper que de moi. (Letter 125, p. 300)

Closing this deal and concluding the bargain that has been awaiting its pay-off since the early stages of the novel will signal a return to the status of lovers they had enjoyed before the novel began.

Mme de Merteuil resists, however. She refuses to sacrifice her projects for the sake of the Vicomte, and she objects to becoming what she calls his "slave" (letter 127, p. 303). She considers herself far superior to all other women, both individually and as a group:

> J'ai pu avoir quelquefois la prétention de remplacer à moi seule tout un sérail. (Letter 127, p. 303)

She rejects his suggestion. Moreover, she claims that he has snubbed and insulted her:

> Mais, autrefois, vous faisiez un peu plus de cas de moi; vous ne m'aviez pas destinée tout à fait aux troisièmes rôles; et surtout vous vouliez bien attendre que j'eusse dit oui, avant d'être sûr de mon consentement. (Letter 127, p. 304)

Merteuil combines here two points essential to the libertine struggle for absolute domination. On one hand, she is most conscious of her own liberty: she refuses to become Valmont's slave and rejects the implication that she be dependent upon him and totally submissive to him. On the other hand, she returns to the question of pride and rivalry that we have already invoked. She is offended by his fascination with the Présidente, since she cannot accept even the suggestion that another woman might be as attractive as she, or that any man, and most especially Valmont, might prefer another woman to herself.

Valmont replies in terms that are most flattering but which are also the common coin of a rake's jargon. He answers both her objections, first chiding her for thinking that "il existât une femme dans le monde, qui me parût préférable à vous" (letter 129, p. 307), then reassuring her of her permanent place in his heart: "que vous êtes, que vous serez toujours, la véritable souveraine de mon cœur" (p. 308).

At this point, the act and the fact of reading make a critical eruption into the novel. Merteuil demands a convincing proof of Valmont's love and affection. In terms of any epistolary novel and in the present context of our interest in the fictional reader, what she asks for is indeed most telling:

> Vous voyez que je m'exécute à mon tour, et cela, sans que vous vous soyez encore mis en règle vis-à-vis de moi: car enfin je devais avoir la première lettre de la céleste prude; et pourtant... je n'ai rien reçu, absolument rien. (Letter 131, p. 312)

Their libertine bargain can be settled and their sexual desires consummated only by this written letter from a third party. At the beginning of this chapter I quoted the original terms of this agreement, with Valmont holding a written pledge of Merteuil's submission (letter 58) and the Marquise promising herself only upon the reception of written proof of the Présidente's downfall (letter 21). By reiterating this demand for written evidence of the Vicomte's sexual conquest, Mme de Merteuil is attempting to maintain the strategic advantage she had previously known as a secret reader spying on Valmont's letters to the Présidente. If she can maintain her presence as an intrusive reader in this ultimate and most personal letter "after the fall," the Marquise will be able to maintain her power over the Vicomte, she will learn from him the minute details of his relation to Mme de Tourvel that will permit her to continue to criticize and denigrate him. What Valmont had willingly, and even thoughtlessly, conceded before, however, he now steadfastly refuses. He attempts to refute Merteuil's suspicions. He denies energetically being in love with Mme de Tourvel and claims that he is only enjoying the glory of his triumph. He allows that the Présidente fascinates him but insists that he is entirely free in his emotions. He loves only the Marquise. Despite such assurances, he chooses to ignore her essential question. He refuses to comment on her demand to become once again his secret, supplementary reader. He would prefer to forget this debt of a letter that he owes her, and along with it, the privileges that Merteuil's reading of Tourvel's letter would necessarily imply. This textual debt, with its sexual price tag marked and clearly expressed in reading and writing values, is nonetheless essential. Valmont and Merteuil will fall out with each other because of these narrative considerations. They are quarreling over narrative as well as sexual matters. Whether he loves Mme de Tourvel or not is less important than determining which of them will become the controlling reader of the Présidente's letter.

Of course these two issues, reading and loving, are inextricably intertwined here as elsewhere in the novel. When Merteuil complains that Valmont does in fact love Mme de Tourvel and prefers the latter to herself, the culminating proof she advances, after having listed a number of items that wound her pride as a woman and a rival, is preeminently a reader's observation:

> Encore dans votre dernière lettre, si vous ne m'y parlez pas de cette femme uniquement, c'est que vous ne voulez me rien dire *de vos grandes affaires*; elles vous semblent si importantes, que le silence que vous gardez sur elles, vous le croyez une punition pour moi. (Letter 141, p. 333, italics in original)

Mentioned or ignored, present or absent, Mme de Tourvel remains so central to Valmont's letters that the Marquise literally reads her existence into the pages even where she does not appear. At the same time and by the same mechanism, she reads into all that Valmont writes his real but repressed love for the Présidente. In desperation, Merteuil warns the Vicomte of the grave danger both of them are courting in words that again emphasize the reader's function and power:

> Prenez-y garde, Vicomte! si une fois je réponds, ma réponse sera irrévocable; et craindre de la faire en ce moment, c'est déjà peut-être en dire trop. Aussi je n'en veux absolument plus parler. (Letter 141, p. 333)

Response is the natural consequence and complement of reading and reception, two of the basic functions which define the reader. But once this reader is pushed beyond her limit, there can be no turning back. Merteuil's anger is too destructive. Once released, it will provoke catastrophe. A narrator like Valmont can speak and write, almost without end, whereas a reader like Merteuil needs to react or to respond but once in order to unleash the final cataclysm. It is only because she is so clever and so manipulative a reader that Merteuil possesses so powerful a weapon. With her dreaded reply she will directly cause the Présidente's death, Valmont's duel and indirectly his death, and finally her own destruction at Danceny's hands. Merteuil is not at all exaggerating when she attributes so much power to her response.

Before turning this deadly weapon against Valmont, and unknowingly against herself, Merteuil prefaces her counterattack with, appropriately, another allusion to the reading process:

> Tout ce que je peux faire, c'est de vous raconter une histoire. Peut-être n'aurez-vous pas le temps de la lire, ou celui d'y faire assez attention pour la bien entendre? libre à vous. (Letter 141, p. 333)

An expert reader herself, the Marquise is warning Valmont that he must read most carefully if he is to understand this anecdote correctly. That is to say, not just its surface meaning (how to break up a love affair), but the deeper implications of the text and of how a text operates. Since the Marquise up to this point has demonstrated her clear superiority as an intelligent and aware reader, she feels justified in considering Valmont diffident and inattentive in that respect. He therefore needs this warning. As ultimate readers of the novel, we too can benefit from Merteuil's subtlety, one of whose minor but provocative touches is that carefully placed question mark.

What follows is the little note that begins:

> On s'ennuie de tout, mon Ange, c'est une loi de la Nature; ce n'est pas ma faute. (Letter 141, p. 333)

and that ends:

> Adieu, mon ange, je t'ai prise avec plaisir, je te quitte sans regret: je te reviendrai peut-être. Ainsi va le monde. Ce n'est pas ma faute. (Letter 141, p. 334)

This cruel and egotistical message exemplifies perfectly the selfish libertine code that has guided both Valmont and Merteuil in all their actions throughout the novel. It rejects human warmth and affection in favor of cold, calculating pleasure; it prefers the negative force of seduction to the positive values of love; and it cynically embodies the self-serving creed of the rake who delights in his own deceptions. And it is here, it seems to me, that Mme de Merteuil wins an impressive victory over Valmont. By giving him this letter which he will forward to Mme de Tourvel, she thwarts him of his narrator's voice, she deprives him of his own words, she robs him of the opportunity to break off with the Présidente in his own manner. He is a perfect receptor: he receives Merteuil's message as a whole and accepts it in its entirety. But "perfect" has the sense of naive and unreflecting. Valmont is utterly transparent and allows Merteuil's message to pass through him to Mme de Tourvel without altering it in the least. This letter is a trap. It is Merteuil's most brilliant counterattack against Valmont and another demonstration of her cleverness as a tactician and reader. Having read the Marquise's message, Valmont proves incapable of modifying it or changing it to fit his own purposes. Merteuil so overwhelms him as he reads her note, that when he becomes in his turn a narrator writing to the Présidente, he cannot find his own voice or choose his own words. For the first time, this excellent narrator whose success with women is based on his genial manipulation of speaking and writing finds himself unable to do anything more than copy what is before him. Without recognizing the ambush so carefully prepared for him, the Vicomte explains how clever he thought it to copy out the *petit modèle épistolaire* that the Marquise provided.

> Ce que je puis vous dire, c'est que ce dernier m'a paru original et propre à faire de l'effet: aussi je l'ai copié tout simplement, et tout simplement encore je l'ai envoyé à la céleste Présidente. (Letter 142, pp. 334-35)

Ironically the letter that finally proves to Mme de Tourvel the truth of her relationship with Valmont was not even written by him. He merely copied it, "simply" as he says. For Valmont, *simplement* is supposed to indicate the speed, dispatch, and detachment of his actions. We might choose to translate it "simplemindedly." Mme de Merteuil speaks through him the words that kill the Présidente. His status as writer or narrator of this climactic letter is so diminished that a separate copy of it does not even appear in the novel. Thanks to Merteuil's ingenious strategy Valmont is robbed of his voice, which is to say, his male status as narrator. The Marquise usurps his narrator's role by overwhelming him when he reads her letter. Mme de Merteuil does then write one of Valmont's most important letters which, despite its crucial value to him, does not figure among the letters attributed to him. Valmont himself disappears as narrator, just as his copy of this text is eclipsed by Merteuil's original version. Merteuil's words, which at first seem to have been addressed to the Vicomte, go in the end to Mme de Tourvel for whom they are really intended. Valmont is nothing more than a carrier, a minimal go-between, a transparent reader who does not realize the full sense of the message he receives and propagates in his turn. He is not even aware of the fatal impact these words will have on the Présidente despite Merteuil's clear warning to *bien entendre*. In addition he fails to perceive the Marquise's ultimate purpose in supplying him with this missive. Technically, Mme de Tourvel becomes a supplementary reader for the first and last time, since it is really Merteuil's letter to Valmont that she reads. Valmont has merely copied it and sent it off to the Présidente. Since this is the only version printed in the novel, it is also the only one that we, the ultimate readers of this novel, have to read. Merteuil is of course fully cognizant of this letter's homicidal power, and she planned it carefully with her secondary reader, Mme de Tourvel, uppermost in her mind. Unprepared for so cruel a letter, Mme de Tourvel is vulnerable to this deadly thrust by an unseen hand. This ruthless gesture is one of the most libertine and immoral acts in the entire novel. It is also a brilliantly conceived and executed maneuver in the war between Valmont and Merteuil by which the apparently passive and defensively oriented female traps and soundly beats the aggressive and attacking male. If Valmont does not at first understand the unfavorable terrain onto which he has been lured, the Marquise explains the situation to him as she unveils her hidden firepower and contemplates the extensive destruction it will wreak:

> vous lui avez envoyé la lettre que je vous avais faite pour elle? En vérité, vous êtes charmant; et vous avez surpassé mon attente! J'avoue de bonne foi que ce triomphe me flatte plus que tous ceux que j'ai pu obtenir jusqu'à présent. . . . mais c'est que ce n'est pas sur elle que j'ai remporté cet avantage; c'est sur vous: voilà le plaisant, et ce qui est vraiment délicieux. (Letter 145, p. 339)

It is as a reader, her own strongest position, that the Marquise combats Valmont, who is strongest as a narrator. Their rivalry as libertines is echoed in this structural opposition. Once she has won her victory, the Marquise can reveal her successful strategy: her eavesdropping and the power she has acquired as a reader. As an extra reader, removed, secret, and occupying a position from which to judge and criticize, she has skillfully manipulated the Vicomte into deserting Mme de Tourvel. The *Adieu* letter is the fatal blow she directed. From Valmont's point of view, to write such a letter is tantamount to delivering a deadly thrust. From Merteuil's perspective, to dictate this note and, what is more important, to oblige Valmont to send it is the result of her painstaking attempt to become the dominant figure through her efforts as a secret reader.

Merteuil cannot believe the extent and ease of her victory, which she clearly understands is more over Valmont, her rival in libertinage, than over the Présidente, who was but the battlefield upon which their conflict was fought. From her vantage point as his most attentive reader, Merteuil has learned Valmont's weaknesses and she exploits this knowledge ruthlessly. She surmises that he does love Mme de Tourvel, but

> parce que je m'amusais à vous en faire honte, vous l'avez bravement sacrifiée. Vous en auriez sacrifié mille, plutôt que de souffrir une plaisanterie. Où nous conduit pourtant la vanité! (Letter 145, p. 340)

And she knows exactly the fatal effect that this letter will have on Mme de Tourvel. Furthermore, she acknowledges, indeed demands, the responsibility for this message which she invented even though Valmont wrote it out and passed it along to the Présidente:

> Vicomte, quand une femme frappe dans le cœur d'une autre, elle manque rarement de trouver l'endroit sensible, et la blessure est incurable. Tandis que je frappais celle-ci [Mme de Tourvel], ou plutôt que je dirigeais vos coups, je n'ai pas oublié que cette femme était ma rivale, que vous l'aviez trouvée préférable à moi, et qu'enfin, vous m'aviez placée au-dessous d'elle. (Letter 145, p. 340)

Merteuil's *petit modèle épistolaire* is therefore a most dangerous weapon which, with one stroke, delivers a mortal blow to the Présidente, her female rival, and demonstrates her superiority as a strategist over Valmont, her rival in libertinage.

Beyond any question of sexual appetites or physical desires, this struggle between Merteuil and the Vicomte is principally an effort to dominate another human being. It concerns the power to lead and to command, the right to think oneself superior and to be obeyed. A few letters earlier, when Valmont resisted Merteuil's suggestions that he was in love with Mme de Tourvel and incapable of breaking with her, the Marquise emphatically expressed her will to dominate and her desire that he serve her:

> Je vous demanderais, au contraire, de continuer ce pénible service [i.e., to remain Cécile's lover, an occupation Valmont is ready to renounce and restore to Danceny], jusqu'à nouvel ordre de ma part; soit que j'aimasse à abuser ainsi de mon empire; soit que, plus indulgente ou plus juste, il me suffît de disposer de vos sentiments, sans vouloir contrarier vos plaisirs. Quoi qu'il en soit, je voudrais être obéie; et mes ordres seraient bien rigoureux! (Letter 134, p. 319)

Mixed with the tone of medieval courtliness[2] (Valmont's *service* to his lady) are echoes of that military metaphor (*empire* and *ordres*). Juxtaposed to Merteuil's flatteringly feminine image of herself as fickle or fanciful (she pretends to abuse her authority or else to be indulgent) is that terrible impression of her as satanically egotistical, self-willed, and determined to dominate. She disposes of Valmont's emotions cavalierly, and most of all, she demands to be obeyed without question or hesitation. Yet this power struggle is most tellingly articulated in terms of reading. Being an intelligent reader and knowing how to beat others by using the knowledge acquired as a reader is the tactic that Mme de Merteuil applies so successfully in her combat with Valmont.

Although he is soundly defeated in the confrontation we have just analyzed, the Vicomte is himself too intelligent not to profit from his own experience as a reader. He was an effective secret reader when he dealt with characters other than the Marquise. Now he confronts her directly, on her chosen terrain. Because Mme de Merteuil has forced him, or rather maneuvered him, into abandoning the Présidente, Valmont retaliates by disturbing the Marquise's liaison with Danceny and by encouraging the latter to return to Cécile. In an early morning letter, he ridicules the Marquise because Danceny did not come to their assignation of the previous evening:

> Hé bien, Marquise, comment vous trouvez-vous des plaisirs de la nuit dernière? n'en êtes-vous pas un peu fatiguée? (Letter 158, p. 365)

Their final and catastrophic battle unfolds along quite symmetrical lines. Opening the endgame, Merteuil destroys Valmont's relationship with the Présidente with the *Adieu, ce n'est pas ma faute* letter. As a countermove, Valmont convinces Danceny to throw over the Marquise, with whom he has recently been infatuated, in order to return to Cécile Volanges. Just as Merteuil exercised the knowledge acquired as a reader to trick the Vicomte into sending Mme de Tourvel that fatal letter, so too does Valmont now employ a reader's gambit against the Marquise. Mocking the contents and imitating the tone of one of her previous letters, he takes full credit for defeating Merteuil's plan to entice Danceny into her secluded lodging and to seduce him:

> Cependant l'amitié qui nous unit, aussi sincère de ma part que bien reconnue de la vôtre, m'a fait désirer, pour vous, l'épreuve de cette nuit; c'est l'ouvrage de mon zèle, il a réussi: mais point de remerciements; cela n'en vaut pas la peine: rien n'était plus facile. (Letter 158, p. 366)

In this libertine battle, not only is victory important, but moreover it should be an elegant victory, brilliantly conceived and executed with ease and a distinctive flair. Still the question remains: how did Valmont do it? The answer: by knowing his reader and by manipulating the letter addressed to that reader, who in this case was the Chevalier. Danceny decided to forgo his nocturnal rendezvous with the Marquise because Cécile wrote to him and, evoking their love, almost promised to make him happy, a traditional phrase in the libertine vocabulary whose suggestive possibilities are meant to entice:

> Depuis quelques jours, Maman n'est jamais chez elle, vous le savez bien; et j'espérais que vous essaieriez de profiter de ce temps de liberté: mais vous ne songez seulement pas à moi; je suis bien malheureuse! . . . Venez donc, mon ami, mon cher ami; que je puisse vous répéter cent fois que je vous aime, que je vous adore, que je n'aimerai jamais que vous. (Letter 156, pp. 362-63)

The temptation is too strong for Danceny. He prefers the chaste although naive love of Cécile to the more experienced sensations that Merteuil offers him. Furthermore, Cécile is his equal, while he cannot but feel inferior to the Marquise. This letter written in Cécile's hand is really a letter of Valmont's, however!

> La lettre que la jeune personne lui à écrite, c'est bien moi qui l'ai dictée. (Letter 158, p. 366)

This war is still a stand-off. Valmont and Merteuil each win a victory over the other, and each suffers a defeat at the other's hands. Victory always goes to the one who has made the best use of the function of reading, the one who has best foreseen and manipulated the ultimate as well as the immediate reader. As if to accent the critical importance of the reading process, so clearly demonstrated in this give-and-take between the Marquise and the Vicomte, Valmont closes his letter with an ironic reflection on the verb *to read*:

> J'espère qu'en y lisant tout ce qu'il [Danceny] voudra, vous y lirez peut-être aussi que les Amants si jeunes ont leurs dangers; et encore, qu'il vaut mieux m'avoir pour ami que pour ennemi. (Letter 158, p. 366)

Thus it seems quite obvious that for these combatants this libertine war to dominate and subjugate others takes place on a literary battlefield and that reading and writing are its principal weapons and tactics.

As a final example, we will briefly recall one more succinct instance of the warring reader and writer. At the bottom of the letter in which the Vicomte demanded that Mme de Merteuil respond and submit to him, she laconically wrote: "Hé bien! la guerre" (letter 153, p. 358). Her refusal is as powerful as it is short. So brief a reply is a most significative gesture, since by making it, she refuses to accept Valmont's letter. By not fulfilling her function as receiver, and by extension keeper, of his letter and by refusing to provide a proper reply, the Marquise rejects both Valmont and his proposal. Her gesture refuses him his status as narrator by breaking off the communicative or narrative circuit. Unilaterally she terminates his privilege to write her, knowing full well how closely it is intertwined with his personality and his success as a rake. Moreover, Merteuil's minimal response is written on his own letter. Not only is his letter rejected and returned to him, but it also fails to elicit a normal and appropriate answer, that is, another letter. Her reply is not a proper response in terms of the expectations of a regular epistolary exchange. Her refusal to keep this letter intended for her and addressed to her marks the final break between these two long-standing correspondents. It is the ultimate insult, the offense that cannot be forgiven. The message itself, "la guerre," clearly denotes the extent of their deteriorating relationship and the growing intensity of their mutual hostility. How accurately the slogan describes this situation: the medium is indeed the message. The reader's refusal to reply correctly or to accept what is addressed to her is in and of itself an opening of hostilities, a declaration of war. This narrative breakdown symbolizes the complete collapse of their personal communications. Form and content combine to depict most effectively their desperate situation. As rivals for the position of supreme libertine, Valmont and Merteuil have finally pronounced the declaration of war that will be irrevocable and ultimately fatal to both of them. Up to this point, the conventions governing reader and writer have been respected. Now they are seriously violated by Merteuil's readerly refusal which destroys the very basis of their epistolary exchanges and the very existence of their personal intimacy. Their mutual self-destruction is made possible, indeed inevitable, by this narrative disintegration.

The Moral Reader

Letters 158 and 159 are the last ones that Valmont and Merteuil write. As both writer and reader, they disappear from the final, culminating pages of this novel which contains one hundred seventy-five letters in all. The definitive resolution of their power struggle lies in others' hands and, what is more significant, in others' words. It is neither surprising nor illogical that the denouement be effected not by the principal actors and initiators but rather by the less active and more subdued personages, by those who read. Just as the struggle between the Marquise and the Vicomte is best articulated by their ruses and maneuvers as readers or as narrators consciously manipulating both their immediate and secondary readers, so too do their separate punishments depend on personages whom we can most accurately describe as readers or receivers.

The novel's resolution is the direct result of a reader's act. Reading rather than sex is the ultimate activity of this novel, and it is reading that establishes the moral vision, the balance, and the revindication that many critics have found wanting in this fiction. A narrator like Valmont might be the most consummate seducer, but in the end a reader triumphs. With that victorious reader, we discover the moral message that Laclos intended his novel to provide.

The most obvious candidate for this role of a reader who imparts a moral lesson is the Chevalier Danceny, whose self-chosen fate as an exiled Knight of Malta offers an appropriately religious background in which to set the moral content of this libertine novel. After having experienced the corruption of the world in Valmont and Merteuil, and after having tasted a bit of its pleasures in his courtship of Mlle de Volanges, Danceny eventually becomes almost a stridently upright and moralizing figure. Not only does he punish the two principal evildoers, but he also devotes the remainder of his life to the expiation of his own faults.

It is thanks to his role as reader that Danceny accomplishes his great work of chastisement and moral restitution. With surprising ease and speed, he punishes both the Vicomte and the Marquise. With his sword, he kills Valmont in a duel; with his pen, he publishes the incriminating letters which directly lead to Merteuil's loss of her reputation, her lawsuit, and her fortune. Both pen and sword are guided and inspired by Danceny's reading. Writing and fighting stem from reading.

That duel was caused when Danceny read Valmont's letters in which the latter bragged of having seduced Cécile. Indignant, the Chevalier wrote to Valmont:

> Je suis instruit, Monsieur, de vos procédés envers moi. (Letter 162, p. 370)

After reading the letters that the dying Valmont confided to him, he is able to publish the truth about Merteuil's humiliation of Prévan and thereby reveal her hypocrisy. The Chevalier earns his role as a force for morality in terms most pertinent to this epistolary novel: by reading letters. Because he has read these letters, he becomes the punisher of iniquity. His personal experience of life and his own involvement in the events retold in the novel do not open his eyes to evil nor do they kindle any moral flame in his breast. His reformation is uniquely the consequence of being an additional reader, an extra receptor beyond the original addressee. His status as a secondary reader resembles the hidden or secret readers discussed earlier. The critical difference is that here Danceny is an open, visible, and acknowledged reader. Thus he terminates the negative connotation of the illegal, secret reader and transforms it into a morally positive role. We can surmise that Mme de Merteuil gave him Valmont's letters about Cécile in order to provoke their duel. Her intention was destructive. Her decision to reveal this secret, personal, and intimate information constitutes another one of her strategic counterattacks in the war between the Vicomte and herself. This strategy, let us repeat, calls upon the reader's function and strength rather than the narrator's. Nevertheless, hers is a Pyrrhic victory since Valmont, dying and defeated, repeats this same gesture. He turns over to Danceny secret documents which will undo Merteuil. With a second round Danceny exacts a morally deserved punishment, this time from the Marquise.

Once admitted to this level of secondary reader, Danceny is transformed into an implacable instrument of destruction. Most significantly, the results of his reading activity are morally satisfying and justified, in marked contrast to the evil wreaked by the other expert secondary readers, Valmont and Merteuil.

Seen then from the perspective of the reader, the punishments inflicted on the Marquise and the Vicomte are symmetrical and equal. The Marquise does not escape justice to continue her life as some incorporal evil essence, as some critics have suggested.[3] Her disfigurement by smallpox and her bankruptcy constitute a death in life that is different from Valmont's actual death but which is intended to be just as definitive. Not the least irony is that Mme de Merteuil and Valmont have succeeded in destroying each other, a feat that no one else could have accomplished, and that the means of their mutual destruction, the hidden reader, was also a principal weapon in their activities as libertines.

Fortunately, Laclos's novel is not as simple nor as easily cut and dried as Danceny's reading role might suggest. There is at least one other moral reader who provides an additional perspective and whose presence complements Danceny's even as it differs from it.

That other super-reader in the closing pages of the novel is Mme de Rosemonde, who achieves this status by a process that parallels Danceny's. We have already discussed her importance as the first fictional reader who can read substantially the same novel that we have before us. In addition we have analyzed her as a "split personality," that is as a character who changes significantly when seen either as a writer or a reader. The present comments should not be interpreted as a contradiction of those preceding remarks; rather such differences should be accepted as attempts to come to grips with the complexities of this multi-leveled novel. Mme de Rosemonde is perched in the fictional margins, one of the last personages/participants whose reading is inscribed inside the novel and simultaneously one of the first readers outside the text whose knowledge and reading of the novel approximate our own. Here we will deal only with her moral function and with its relationship to her very special status as a reader.

Despite an initial impulse, soon forgotten, to bring Valmont's adversary to justice, Mme de Rosemonde is no instrument of vengeance. Unlike Danceny, she does not feel it her duty to expose these evildoers and to punish them. On the contrary, she sounds a note of forgiveness. Crushed by the revelations about her beloved nephew, she cannot bring herself to judge him harshly or unkindly. Even though she recognizes the evil he has done, she refuses to see any justice in his death. Mme de Rosemonde's final judgment is gentle indeed for the man who so cruelly betrayed Mme de Tourvel, her close friend whose death in a frenzy of self-incrimination and mental imbalance she practically witnessed through Mme de Volanges's letters. If there is a villain in her eyes, it is the Marquise de Merteuil. Nor does she hesitate to remind Danceny of his own less than honorable part in Cécile's downfall:

> car enfin, quelque illusion qu'on cherche à se faire par une prétendue délicatesse de sentiments, celui qui le premier tente de séduire un cœur encore honnête et simple se rend par là même le premier fauteur de sa corruption, et doit être à jamais comptable des égarements et des excès qui la suivent. (Letter 171, p. 387)

Perhaps she emphasizes the evil done by Merteuil and Danceny so as to lessen Valmont's guilt. Be that as it may, in contrast to the strict justice of the Chevalier's hand which punishes Valmont and Merteuil's sins by the very means of their sinning, Mme de Rosemonde invokes a charity that almost neglects to recognize the one principally responsible for doing all this evil. To Danceny's indispensable function as the protector of moral and societal responsibilities, Laclos adds the compassionate Rosemonde. This ambiguous juxtaposition helps explain the critics' perplexity over the moral message of the *Liaisons dangereuses*. Like Danceny, we feel impelled to agree and even to demand that wrongs be righted and the guilty be punished, while we also share with Mme de Rosemonde an inexplicable yet invincible attraction towards at least one of those wicked characters who fully deserve the punishment they suffer.

The alternatives and the contradictions presented by these two final readers inform the ambivalent, fascinating, and distinctly modern conclusion to this novel. Such an open ending leaves each of us to resolve our own feelings based on suggestions and models within the text, but at the same time does not compel us to embrace one reaction rather than another. By not definitively fixing all the issues, this same open ending returns us to our concern with the fictional reader and the reading process. Reading is the key ongoing activity both inside this novel and outside it. Hard and fast conclusions are less important than our awareness that the fiction's own logic and structure can produce a continual *remise en question* and justify yet another re-reading.

As the novel closes with Mme de Rosemonde at center stage, either as one moralizing viewpoint or simply as the sole collector of the various correspondences, we are led in circular fashion to think once again about her curious relationship with those two marginal figures, the *rédacteur* and the *éditeur*, who opened the novel with their prefaces about how they acquired the letters they were publishing. The more closely we examine that relationship, however, the more ambiguous and contradictory it becomes. At the very outset the *rédacteur* claimed to have been commissioned to produce this volume of letters:

> Cet ouvrage, ou plutôt ce recueil, que le public trouvera peut-être encore trop volumineux, ne contient pourtant que le plus petit nombre des lettres qui composaient la totalité de la correspondance dont il est extrait. Chargé de la mettre en ordre par les personnes à qui elle était parvenue, et que je savais dans l'intention de la publier, je n'ai demandé, pour prix de mes soins, que la permission d'élaguer tout ce qui me paraîtrait inutile. (Préface du Rédacteur, p. 3)

By the novel's end, however, we know that the *rédacteur* is not referring to Mme de Rosemonde here. First of all, he mentions several individuals who want to publish these letters. That plural *personnes* cannot designate her. Moreover the original, authentic letters belong to these several persons who have inherited them, a detail casually mentioned in a footnote: "les originaux subsistent entre les mains des héritiers de Mme de Rosemonde" (letter 169, note, p. 382). The *rédacteur*'s claim that these heirs chose to publish the letters runs counter to Mme de Rosemonde's own wishes. She herself stated that she wanted to leave all these letters to gather dust, unknown and unseen by other eyes:

> Je me prêterai volontiers, Monsieur, pour ce qui me concerne, à laisser dans le silence et l'oubli tout ce qui pourrait avoir trait et donner suite à ces tristes événements. (Letter 171, p. 386)

What she says to Danceny she repeats to Mme de Volanges, so there can be little doubt that she really intends to allow no one else to look at and to read these letters:

> la grâce qui me reste à vous demander, ma chère amie, est de ne plus m'interroger sur rien qui ait rapport à ces tristes événements: laissons-les dans l'oubli qui leur convient. (Letter 172, p. 388)

That connection between the editors and Mme de Rosemonde which seemed so right at the beginning of the novel turns out to be wrong at the end. There is in fact no direct link between Mme de Rosemonde, the ultimate fictional reader, and those editors, the ultimate fictional narrators in the loosest definition of that term. The point of contact between these fictional emitters of the novel, located just on the margins of the fiction itself, and that fictive receiver inside the novel has been erased in the course of the very story of which they are a part.

The movement of letters from reader to reader through a chain of fictional readings is a critical element of the *Liaisons dangereuses*. However, this structural logic disintegrates at the (illusory!) point of contact between Mme de Rosemonde and the editors. That juncture which once appeared so natural as to require no elaborate discussion now reveals its problematic nature. Latent ever since the opening pages of the novel, this inconsistency finally springs its trap and impells us, as readers ourselves, to reflect once again upon the critical nature of reading and receiving, of accepting letters, of keeping them, and of sending them on to other readers. In this cleverly invented divergence rather than convergence between reader and writer, the communication model that has guided our reading of the novel is turned on its head. A last complication arises in determining who is the addresser here and who the addressee: the editors could be considered Rosemonde's receivers since she sends them the letters in question, albeit indirectly. With this ironic parting shot we hear a ludic echo of our interest in the act of reading and in those intimate, intrusive, and triumphant personages who are the fictional readers in the *Liaisons dangereuses*.

Notes

Preface: Pentecost: The Feast of the Reader

[1] Acts 2.1-12, King James Version.

[2] Jerusalem Bible translation, verse 8.

[3] King James Version, verse 12.

[4] Martin Turnell, *The Novel in France* (New York: New Directions, 1951), p. 51: "Laclos let the cat out of the bag," a revelation that showed how corrupt French society really was and thus constituted the "immense *trahison*."

[5] Fernand Caussy, *Laclos 1741-1803* (Paris: Mercure de France, 1905), offers a full biography along with an effort to identify the real names behind the *clés*. Thus, for example, the Marquise de Merteuil would be a Marquise de L.T.D.P.M. or the Marquise de Montmort while Prévan is a M. de Rochechouart (p. 29). Claude Manceron also offers a few identifications in his *Le Bon Plaisir 1782-1785*, the third volume of his massive history, *Les Hommes de la Liberté* (Paris: Robert Laffont, 1976), pp. 100-08.

[6] Throughout this study, I will use several terms to refer to this fictional reader. The most common will be "reader" or "fictional reader," since those words are the most conclusive and encompassing. On occasion I will employ other terms in the critical lexicon like addressee, narratee, recipient, or receiver. I would hope that choosing one word over another would indicate a shade of meaning or a nuance within that larger concept of the intradiegetic reader, the fictive personage whose very act of reading is an integral part of the fiction itself.

[7] I am fully aware of my own subjectivity even as I search for critical objectivity, a paradoxical situation brilliantly discussed by Serge Doubrovsky, *The New Criticism in France,* trans. Derek Coltman (Chicago: University of Chicago Press, 1973), especially Chapter vi, "Criticism as Phenomenology," pp. 122-32.

Chapter 1: Introduction to the Fictional Reader

[1] Gerald Prince, "Introduction à l'étude du narrataire," *Poétique,* 14 (Oct. 1973), 177-96.

[2] See W. Daniel Wilson, "Readers in Texts," *PMLA*, 96, No. 5 (Oct. 1981), 848-63, for a discussion of German equivalents: *fiktiver Leser, intendierter Leser*.

[3] Roman Jakobson, "Linguistique et poétique," in *Essais de linguistique générale* (Paris: Editions du Seuil, 1963), pp. 209-49. The original English version is "Closing Statements: Linguistics and Poetics," in *Style in Language*, ed. Thomas Seboek (Boston: MIT Press, 1960).

[4] Emile Benveniste, *Problèmes de linguistique générale* (Paris: Gallimard, 1966).

[5] Susan Sniader Lanser, *The Narrative Act: Point of View in Prose Fiction* (Princeton: Princeton University Press, 1981).

[6] Seymour Chatman, *Story and Discourse: Narrative Structure in Fiction and Film* (Ithaca, N.Y.: Cornell University Press, 1978).

[7] Lanser, p. 133, footnote.

[8] Jean Rousset, "La Monodie épistolaire: Crébillon fils," *Etudes Littéraires*, 1 (1968), 167-74.

[9] Of course, there are many other definitions of the "reader" and each one implies a different critical orientation and approach to the text. In addition to W. Daniel Wilson's article cited above, see especially the sampler of "reader-response" criticism edited by Jane Tompkins, *Reader-Response Criticism: From Formalism to Post-Structuralism* (Baltimore: Johns Hopkins University Press, 1980). As valid as these other approaches to the reader may be, they are not mine: here I will discuss only fictional readers.

[10] For a good general discussion and résumé of this question, see Ronald Rosbottom, *Choderlos de Laclos*, TWAS, No. 502 (Boston: Twayne Publishers, 1978), especially pp. 93-113.

[11] Hawthorne's elaborate explanation/justification of his editorial rather than authorial role is given in "The Custom-House," the long preface to the novel; long is not an exaggeration since it runs to about one-fifth of the novel's length.

[12] For an interesting new angle on such sentimental reading, see Robert Darnton, "Readers Respond to Rousseau: The Fabrication of Romantic Sensitivity," *The Great Cat Massacre* (New York: Basic Books, 1984), pp. 215-56.

[13] Frédéric Deloffre, "L'Enigme des *Lettres portugaises*," in his edition of Guilleragues, *Les Lettres portugaises* (Paris: Garnier Frères, 1962), pp. v-xxiii.

[14] Georges Roth, "Histoire d'un manuscrit et d'un texte," in his edition of Françoise d'Epinay, *Histoire de Madame de Montbrillant* (Paris: Gallimard, 1951), I, vii-xlii. Roth's judicious attitude and scholarly evenhandedness almost confuse the issue, since he seems to support, in different places, both views, i.e., that the *Histoire* is a novel and an autobiography: ". . . Mme d'Epinay a finalement composé un roman à clé, long récit à base autobiographique où elle s'est mise en scène sous le nom de son héroïne, où Jean-Jacques figure sous celui de 'René,' où Diderot s'appelle 'Garnier,' où Grimm devient 'Volx,' et où tous les autres acteurs, parents, amis et relations, portent aussi des noms fictifs.

Mais bien que la trame du récit repose sur un fonds partiellement véritable, les noms de fantaisie attribués aux personnages maintiennent à la narratrice ses droits de romancière—dont elle a usé. Dans quelle exacte proportion? Impossible de le déterminer avec une certitude rigoureuse. . . . Seul l'écrivain pourrait le dire—au moment même où il écrit. Car ensuite lui-même devient sa propre dupe. . . . Où se limite l'autobiographie, où commence la fiction?" (pp. xi-xii). Before Roth, most readers and editors accepted this text as historically accurate memoirs and not as fiction, an error still perpetrated by some libraries where it is catalogued under history (Library of Congress classification: DC) rather than literature (PQ).

[15] Elisabeth Badinter, *Emilie, Emilie: L'Ambition féminine au XVIIIe siècle* (Paris: Flammarion, 1983). See, for example, a comment like: "Selon toute probabilité, elle commença d'écrire son roman, *Madame de Montbrillant,* qui n'était autre que son histoire, dans les années 1756-1757 . . ." (p. 356).

[16] Of course, the very idea of being "right" or "wrong" is foolish here since both sides belong to a fictional universe where the issue is not one side vs. the other but rather the play, the tension between them.

[17] Choderlos de Laclos, *Les Liaisons dangereuses,* édition de Y. Le Hir (Paris: Garnier Frères, 1961). All subsequent citations will be made to this edition with both the letter and the page number indicated parenthetically in the text.

[18] On the question of narrative techniques, see Vivienne Mylne, *The Eighteenth-Century French Novel: Techniques of Illusion* (Manchester, Eng.: Manchester University Press, 1965). Written over twenty years ago, this book has lost none of its value. In fact, it has just recently been reprinted by Cambridge University Press (1981).

[19] See, for example, Yvon Belaval, *Choderlos de Laclos* (Paris: Seghers, 1972), p. 37: "Les lettres des romans imitent les lettres réelles. Les lettres des *Liaisons dangereuses* les imitent si bien que l'on ose à peine décider si elles sont d'imagination ou réelles."

[20] Eugène Vaillé, *Histoire générale des postes françaises* (Paris: Presses Universitaires Françaises, 1949), II, 190.

[21] Vaillé, II, 190.

[22] Vaillé, V, 109.

[23] The connection between the rise of the bourgeoisie and the ascendancy of the novel as a literary genre has been made often enough to justify the use of the adjective *bourgeois* here and to explain the pertinence of that term to our discussion. The classic analysis of the relationship between the bourgeoisie and the novel is *The Rise of the Novel,* by Ian Watt (1957; rpt. Berkeley: University of California Press, 1967).

[24] See one outstanding exception, however: Janet Altman, "Addressed and Undressed Language in *Les Liaisons dangereuses,*" in *Laclos: Critical Approaches to "Les Liaisons dangereuses,"* ed. Lloyd Free (Madrid: Porrúa, 1978), pp. 223-57.

[25] Jean-Luc Seylaz, *"Les Liaisons dangereuses" et la création romanesque chez Laclos* (Genève: Droz, 1958), pp. 23 and 111.

Chapter 2: A Theory of Fictional Readers and Their Reading

[1] Georges Daniel, *Fatalité du secret et fatalité du bavardage au XVIIIe siècle* (Paris: A.-G. Nizet, 1966), p. 16.

[2] Of course, the primary sense is physical lovemaking here, although other, "higher" implications cannot be excluded, especially in this context of friendship and confidentiality. Nonetheless, just as their confidence in each other ebbs, so too does the full sense of the word *love*.

[3] See, for example, Rosbottom, p. 82: "writing a letter is an act of recognition which demands recognition in return"; and p. 99: "reading presupposes writing; a letter does not in effect fulfill its function unless and until it is read."

[4] See René Pomeau, *Laclos* (Paris: Hatier, 1975), p. 71: "La technique du roman par lettres apparaît ici consubstantielle à la matière romanesque"; and p. 72: "Le tissu même du roman est ainsi constitué par la production et la circulation des missives."

[5] See Seylaz, pp. 19-20: "L'originalité de Laclos, c'est d'avoir donné une valeur dramatique à la composition par lettres, d'avoir fait de ces lettres l'étoffe même du roman et d'avoir réalisé ainsi, entre le sujet du livre et le mode de narration un accord si étroit que ce mode en devient non seulement vraisemblable mais nécessaire."

[6] See my own article, "Real Fiction: Authenticity in the French Epistolary Novel," *Romanic Review*, 72, No. 4 (Nov. 1981), 409-24.

[7] The classic statement of this fact is Emile Benveniste, *Problèmes de linguistique générale* (Paris: Gallimard, 1966), p. 260.

[8] Tzvetan Todorov, "Les Catégories du récit littéraire," *Communications*, 8 (1966), p. 147.

[9] Françoise Meltzer, "Laclos' Purloined Letters," *Critical Inquiry*, 8, No. 3 (Summer 1982), 517: "The role of the reader is central to the epistolary genre because the letters anticipate a reader within the novel's framework. . . . And yet it is in the novel of letters that the reader, the fictional reader, most clearly creates the text."

[10] Meltzer, p. 519: "The letters themselves, I am arguing, can also be regarded as signifiers in the way, the most superficial way, Lacan describes."

[11] See Godfrey F. Singer, *The Epistolary Novel* (New York: Russell and Russell, 1963), pp. 136-37: "On the other hand, there is no real characterization in this novel; there is a flood of endless repetition to be found in it; the carrying on of a correspondence between people in the very same castle deprives the book of verisimilitude, and practically nothing at all happens with an almost romantic monotony."

[12] Our analysis thus gives a new argument to those who maintain that Valmont commits a form of suicide in dueling with Danceny. For Valmont's suicide, see Daniel, pp. 88-89.

Chapter 3: Hidden Readers

[1] See Henri Duranton, "*Les Liaisons dangereuses* ou le miroir ennemi," *Revue des Sciences Humaines*, 153 (1974), 125-43.

[2] See Altman, p. 225: "in the *Liaisons*, narrative is always refracted through two prisms: what is said is as much a function of the addressee as the writer."

[3] For an analysis that picks up some of the points which I am emphasizing here but which also places them in a militant feminist perspective, see Nancy Miller, "Rereading as a Woman: The Body in Practice," *Poetics Today*, 6, Nos. 1-2 (1985), 291-99. This essay appears in a special issue entitled "The Female Body in Western Culture: Semiotic Perspectives."

[4] On Laclos's debt to the theater, see the amazingly comprehensive work of Laurent Versini, *Laclos et la tradition: Essai sur les sources et la technique des "Liaisons dangereuses"* (Paris: Klincksieck, 1968), pp. 215-30. Valmont even calls Azolan "un vrai valet de comédie" (letter 15, p. 35).

[5] Although the exact dosage remains in dispute, there can be little doubt that Laclos did have this social phenomenon in mind. Pomeau argues against this kind of social realism (pp. 163-64), while Roger Vailland in his *Laclos par lui-même* (Paris: Editions du Seuil, 1953) argues in favor of it.

[6] On the delicate question of Mme de Merteuil's femininity and/or virility, see Nancy Miller, *The Heroine's Text: Readings in the French and English Novel 1722-1782* (New York: Columbia University Press, 1980), p. 136: "She attempts to be a male hero . . ."; and p. 145: "By usurping the male prerogative of *attack*, Merteuil becomes guilty of female depravity."

[7] Earlier we noted that Valmont's hand participated in his own death by writing the incriminating letter; here the Marquise's hand, by handing over this letter to Danceny, is also a causal factor. These are not contradictions, but rather the rich complexity of Laclos's novel that our interest in the reader makes more evident.

[8] I am currently at work on an essay analyzing the sexual ideology that Laclos depicts in his novel, entitled "Male Bonding and Female Isolation."

[9] See, for example, Pomeau, pp. 67-69. For the eighteenth century's belief about the immorality of this denouement, see La Harpe's comments quoted in Maurice Allem's edition of Laclos's *Œuvres complètes* (Paris: Gallimard, 1951), p. 704: "Le vice ne trouve donc pas ici sa punition en lui-même, et ce dénouement sans moralité ne vaut pas mieux que le reste." On the other hand, Christine Belcikowski in her *Poétique des "Liaisons dangereuses"* (Paris: José Corti, 1972) says: "C'est le dénouement qui sert de clef de voûte à l'édifice du roman" (p. 18).

[10] In contrast Aram Vartanian explains Merteuil's success by emphasizing her masculine rather than feminine qualities in his "The Marquise de Merteuil: A Case of Mistaken Identity," *L'Esprit Créateur* 3 (1963), 172-80.

Chapter 4: Split Personalities: Characterizing Writers and Readers

[1] See Yves Le Hir, "La Langue et le style," in his introduction to *Les Liaisons dangereuses* (Paris: Garnier Frères, 1961), pp. xxi-l.

Chapter 5: Writer vs. Reader: The Struggle for Power

[1] Bussy-Rabutin's *Histoire amoureuse des Gaules* (1665) stands out as one of the most complete and detailed expressions of this conceit that love is a war and that every amorous activity can be described by a military metaphor. It remained a major source and inspiration for the licentious novelists of the eighteenth century.

[2] See Lloyd Free, "Laclos and the Myth of Courtly Love," *Studies on Voltaire and the Eighteenth Century,* 148 (1976), 201-23.

[3] For example, Pierre Fauchery, *La Destinée féminine dans le roman européen du XVIIIe siècle: 1713-1807* (Paris: Armand Colin, 1972), pp. 674-75.

Selected Bibliography

The following bibliography makes no pretense to being exhaustive. Rather, it is a selected and personal choice of those articles and books which I have found helpful, either in establishing the critical principles most useful for studying the idea of a fictional reader, or else in analyzing the *Liaisons dangereuses* and in dealing with the multiple questions of its structure, its characterizations, and its art as a novel.

The Text

Choderlos de Laclos, Pierre-Ambroise-François. *Les Liaisons dangereuses*. Edition de Y. Le Hir. Paris: Garnier Frères, 1961.

———. *Œuvres complètes*. Texte établi et annoté par Maurice Allem. Bibliothèque de la Pléiade. Paris: Gallimard, 1951.

———. *Œuvres complètes*. Texte établi, présenté et annoté par Laurent Versini. Bibliothèque de la Pléiade. Paris: Gallimard, 1979.

Secondary Readings

Altman, Janet. "Addressed and Undressed Language in *Les Liaisons dangereuses*." In *Laclos: Critical Approaches to "Les Liaisons dangereuses."* Ed. Lloyd Free. Madrid: Porrúa, 1978, pp. 223-57.

———. *Epistolarity: Approaches to a Form*. Columbus: Ohio State University Press, 1982.

———. "The 'Triple Register': Introduction to Temporal Complexity in the Letter-Novel." *L'Esprit Créateur,* 17 (1977), 302-10.

Anderson, Howard, Philip Daghlian, and Irvin Ehrenpreis, eds. *The Familiar Letter in the Eighteenth Century*. Lawrence: University Press of Kansas, 1968.

Badinter, Elisabeth. *Emilie, Emilie: L'Ambition féminine au XVIIIe siècle.* Paris: Flammarion, 1983.

Bal, Mieke. "Narration et focalisation: Pour une théorie des instances du récit." *Poétique,* 29 (1977), 107-27.

———. *Narratologie: Essais sur la signification narrative dans quatre romans modernes.* Paris: Klincksieck, 1977.

Bann, Stephen, and John E. Bowlt, eds. *Russian Formalism.* New York: Barnes and Noble, 1973.

Barguillet, Françoise. *Le Roman au XVIIIe siècle.* Paris: Presses Universitaires de France, 1981.

Barthes, Roland. *Le Degré zéro de l'écriture.* Bibliothèque Médiations 40. Paris: Gonthier, 1969.

———. *Essais critiques.* Collection Tel Quel. Paris: Editions du Seuil, 1964.

———. *Image-Music-Text.* Trans. Stephan Heath. New York: Hill and Wang, 1981.

———. "Introduction à l'analyse structurale des récits." *Communications,* 8 (1966), 1-27.

———. *Le Plaisir du texte.* Collection Tel Quel. Paris: Editions du Seuil, 1973.

———. *S/Z.* Collection Points. Paris: Editions du Seuil, 1970.

Batlay, Jenny. "Amour et métaphore: Analyse de la lettre 23 des *Liaisons dangereuses.*" *Studies on Voltaire and the Eighteenth Century,* 117 (1974), 251-57.

Belaval, Yvon. *Choderlos de Laclos.* Ecrivains d'Hier et d'Aujourd'hui 40. Paris: Seghers, 1972.

Belcikowski, Christine. *Poétique des "Liaisons dangereuses."* Paris: José Corti, 1972.

Benveniste, Emile. *Problèmes de linguistique générale.* Paris: Gallimard, 1966.

Beugnot, Bernard. "Débats autour du genre épistolaire." *Revue d'Histoire Littéraire de la France,* 74, No. 2 (1974), 195-202.

Blanc, Henri. *"Les Liaisons dangereuses" de Choderlos de Laclos.* Poche Critique. Paris: Hachette, 1972.

Bourgeac, Jacques. "A partir de la lettre 48 des *Liaisons dangereuses*: Analyse stylistique." *Studies on Voltaire and the Eighteenth Century,* 183 (1979), 177-88.

Boyer, Henri. "Structuration d'un roman épistolaire: Enonciation et fiction." *Revue des Langues Romanes,* 80 (1972), 297-327.

Selected Bibliography

Brooks, Peter. *The Novel of Worldliness.* Princeton: Princeton University Press, 1969.

Carrell, Susan Lee. *Le Soliloque de la passion féminine ou le dialogue illusoire.* Etudes Littéraires Françaises 12. Paris: Editions Jean-Michel Place, 1982.

Caussy, Fernand. *Laclos 1741-1803.* Paris: Mercure de France, 1905.

Champagne, Roland. "The Spiralling Discourse: Todorov's Model for a Narratology in *Les Liaisons dangereuses.*" *L'Esprit Créateur,* 14 (1974), 342-52.

Chatman, Seymour. *Story and Discourse: Narrative Structure in Fiction and Film.* Ithaca, N.Y.: Cornell University Press, 1978.

Cherpack, Clifton. "A New Look at the *Liaisons dangereuses.*" *Modern Language Notes,* 74 (1959), 513-21.

Conroy, Peter V., Jr. "Image claire, image trouble dans la *Grecque moderne* de Prévost." *Studies on Voltaire and the Eighteenth Century,* 217 (1983), 187-97.

———. "Real Fiction: Authenticity in the French Epistolary Novel." *Romanic Review,* 72, No. 4 (Nov. 1981), 409-24.

Coulet, Henri. "Les Lettres occultées des *Liaisons dangereuses.*" *Revue d'Histoire Littéraire de la France,* 82, No. 4 (July-Aug. 1982), 600-14. This entire issue is devoted to Laclos.

———. *Le Roman jusqu'à la Révolution.* Paris: Armand Colin, 1967.

Coward, D. A. "Laclos and the 'dénouement' of the *Liaisons dangereuses.*" *Eighteenth-Century Studies,* 5 (1972), 431-49.

Culler, Jonathan. *The Pursuit of Signs: Semiotics, Literature, Deconstruction.* Ithaca, N.Y.: Cornell University Press, 1981.

———. *Structuralist Poetics: Structuralism, Linguistics, and the Study of Literature.* Ithaca, N.Y.: Cornell University Press, 1975.

Dagen, Jean. "D'une logique de l'écriture: *Les Liaisons dangereuses.*" *Littératures,* 4 (Autumn 1981), 33-52.

Daniel, Georges. *Fatalité du secret et fatalité du bavardage au XVIIIe siècle: La Marquise de Merteuil. Jean-François Rameau.* Paris: A.-G. Nizet, 1966.

Darnton, Robert. *The Great Cat Massacre and Other Episodes in French Cultural History.* New York: Basic Books, 1984.

Delmas, André, and Yvette Delmas. *A la recherche des "Liaisons dangereuses."* Paris: Mercure de France, 1964.

de Man, Paul. *Allegories of Reading: Figural Language in Rousseau, Nietzsche, Rilke, and Proust.* New Haven: Yale University Press, 1979.

Derrida, Jacques. *De la grammatologie.* Collection Critique. Paris: Editions de Minuit, 1967.

Diaconoff, Suellen. *Eros and Power in "Les Liaisons dangereuses": A Study in Evil.* Genève: Droz, 1978.

Doubrovsky, Serge. *The New Criticism in France.* Trans. Derek Coltman. Chicago: University of Chicago Press, 1973.

Duchêne, Roger. "Du destinataire au public, ou les métamorphoses d'une correspondance privée." *Revue d'Histoire Littéraire de la France,* 76, No. 1 (1976), 29-46.

Ducot, Oswald. *Le Structuralisme en linguistique.* Collection Points. Paris: Editions du Seuil, 1968.

Dunn, Susan. "Education and Seduction in *Les Liaisons dangereuses.*" *Symposium,* 34 (1980), 125-37.

Duranton, Henri. "*Les Liaisons dangereuses* ou le miroir ennemi." *Revue des Sciences Humaines,* 153 (1974), 125-43.

Eagleton, Terry. *Literary Theory.* Minneapolis: University of Minnesota Press, 1983.

Eco, Umberto. *The Role of the Reader: Explorations in the Semiotics of Texts.* A Midland Book MB-318. Bloomington: Indiana University Press, 1984.

———. *A Theory of Semiotics.* A Midland Book MB-217. Bloomington: Indiana University Press, 1979.

Edmiston, William. "The Role of the Listener: Narrative Technique in Diderot's *Ceci n'est pas un conte.*" *Diderot Studies,* 20 (1981), 61-75.

Epinay, Françoise d'. *Histoire de Madame de Montbrillant: Les Pseudo-Mémoires de Madame d'Epinay.* Ed. Georges Roth. 3 vols. Paris: Gallimard, 1951.

"Epistolary Literature of the Eighteenth Century." *L'Esprit Créateur,* 17 (Winter 1977). The entire volume is devoted to the epistolary novel in the eighteenth century. Articles of particular importance will also be listed separately under their respective authors.

Erlich, Victor. *Russian Formalism: History-Doctrine.* 3rd ed. New Haven: Yale University Press, 1981.

Fabre, Jean. "*Les Liaisons dangereuses,* roman de l'ironie." In *Missions et démarches de la critique: Mélanges offerts au professeur J. A. Vier.* Paris: Klincksiek, 1973.

Faye, Jean-Pierre. *Théorie du récit: Introduction aux "langages totalitaires."* Collection Savoir. Paris: Hermann, 1972.

Fish, Stanley. *Is There a Text in This Class? The Authority of Interpretive Communities.* Cambridge: Harvard University Press, 1980.

Free, Lloyd. "Crébillon fils, Laclos, and the Code of the Libertine." *Eighteenth-Century Life,* 1 (1974), 36-40.

———. "Laclos and the Myth of Courtly Love." *Studies on Voltaire and the Eighteenth Century,* 148 (1976), 201-23.

———, ed. *Laclos: Critical Approaches to "Les Liaisons dangereuses."* Madrid: Porrúa, 1978.

Genette, Gérard. *Figures III.* Collection Poétique. Paris: Editions du Seuil, 1972.

Gillis, Christina Marsden. *The Paradox of Privacy: Epistolary Form in "Clarissa."* Gainesville: University Presses of Florida, 1984.

Girard, René. *Deceit, Desire, and the Novel: Self and Other in Literary Structures.* Trans. Yvonne Freccero. Baltimore: Johns Hopkins University Press, 1965.

Giraudoux, Jean. *Littérature.* Paris: Gallimard, 1967.

Godel, Robert, ed. *A Geneva School Reader in Linguistics.* Bloomington: Indiana University Press, 1969.

Goulemot, Jean Marie. "Le Lecteur-voyeur et la mise en scène de l'imaginaire viril dans *Les Liaisons dangereuses.*" In *Laclos et le libertinage.* Ed. René Pomeau and Laurent Versini. Paris: Presses Universitaires de France, 1983, pp. 163-75.

Gutwirth, Madelyn. "Laclos and 'Le Sexe': The Rock of Ambivalence." *Studies on Voltaire and the Eighteenth Century,* 189 (1979), 247-96.

Harari, Josué, ed. *Textual Strategies: Perspectives in Post-Structuralist Criticism.* Ithaca, N.Y.: Cornell University Press, 1979.

Hartman, Geoffrey H. *Criticism in the Wilderness: The Study of Literature Today.* New Haven: Yale University Press, 1980.

———. *Saving the Text: Literature/Derrida/Philosophy.* Baltimore: Johns Hopkins University Press, 1981.

Heuvel, Pierre van den. "Le Narrateur narrataire ou le narrateur lecteur de son propre discours." *Agora,* 14-15 (1977), 53-77.

Hutcheon, Linda. *Narcissistic Narrative: The Metafictional Paradox.* Waterloo, Ont.: Wilfrid Laurier University Press, 1980.

Hydak, Michael G. "La Liaison la plus dangereuse." *Romanica,* 20 (1978-79), 136-38.

Iser, Wolfgang. *The Implied Reader: Patterns of Communication in Prose Fiction from Bunyan to Beckett.* Baltimore: Johns Hopkins Universtiy Press, 1974.

Jakobson, Roman. *Essais de linguistque générale.* Collection Points 17. Paris: Editions du Seuil, 1963.

Jameson, Fredric. *Marxism and Form: Twentieth-Century Dialectical Theories of Literature.* Princeton: Princeton University Press, 1971.

———. *The Prison House of Language.* Princeton: Princeton University Press, 1972.

Jauss, Hans Robert. *Aesthetic Experience and Literary Hermeneutics.* Trans. Michael Shaw. Minneapolis: University of Minnesota Press, 1982.

———. *Toward an Aesthetic of Reception.* Trans. Timothy Bahti. Minneapolis: University of Minnesota Press, 1983.

Jones, Shirley. "Literary and Philosophical Elements in *Les Liaisons dangereuses*: The Case of Merteuil." *French Studies,* 38, No. 2 (Apr. 1984), 159-69.

Jost, François. "L'Evolution d'un genre: Le Roman épistolaire dans les lettres occidentales." In *Essais de Littérature Comparée.* Urbana: University of Illinois Press, 1969, II, 89-179.

Kars, Hendrik. *Le Portrait chez Marivaux: Etude d'un type de segment textuel.* Amsterdam: Rodopi, 1981.

Katz, Eve. "Ambiguity in *Les Liaisons dangereuses.*" *Forum for Modern Language Studies,* 10 (1974), 121-29.

Lanser, Susan Sniader. *The Narrative Act: Point of View in Prose Fiction.* Princeton: Princeton University Press, 1981.

Laufer, Roger. *Style Rococo, Style des "Lumières."* Paris: José Corti, 1963.

Lee, Vera. "Decoding Letter 50 in *Les Liaisons dangereuses.*" *Romance Notes,* 10 (1979), 304-09.

Lemieux, Raymond. "Valmont, libertin amoureux ou homme à projet?" *Romance Notes,* 20 (1980), 349-54.

Lentricchia, Frank. *After the New Criticism.* Chicago: University of Chicago Press, 1980.

Macksey, Richard, and Eugenio Donato, eds. *The Structuralist Controversy: The Languages of Criticism and the Sciences of Man.* Baltimore: Johns Hopkins University Press, 1972.

Malraux, André. *Le Triangle noir.* 1939; rpt. Paris: Gallimard, 1970.

Martindale, Colin. "Structural Balance and the Rules of Narrative in *Les Liaisons dangereuses.*" *Poetics,* 5 (1976), 57-63.

Mason, Haydn. "*Les Liaisons dangereuses*: A Tract for the Times?" *Forum* [Houston, Tex.], 16 (1978), 35-41.

Masseau, Didier. "Le Narrataire des *Liaisons dangereuses.*" In *Laclos et le libertinage.* Ed. René Pomeau and Laurent Versini. Paris: Presses Universitaires de France, 1983, pp. 111-35.

Selected Bibliography

May, Georges. *Le Dilemme du roman au XVIIIe siècle*. Paris: Presses Universitaires de France, 1963.

———. "The Witticisms of Monsieur de Valmont." *L'Esprit Créateur*, 3 (1963), 181-87.

Meltzer, Françoise. "Laclos' Purloined Letters." *Critical Inquiry*, 8, No. 3 (Spring 1982), 515-29.

Miller, Nancy. "Female Sexuality and Narrative Structure in *La Nouvelle Héloïse* and *Les Liaisons dangereuses.*" *Signs*, 1 (1976), 609-38.

———. *The Heroine's Text: Readings in the French and English Novel 1722-1782*. New York: Columbia University Press, 1980.

———. "Rereading as a Woman: The Body in Practice." *Poetics Today*, 6, Nos. 1-2 (1985), 291-99.

Mitchell, W. J. T., ed. *On Narrative*. Chicago: University of Chicago Press, 1981. Reprints of articles from *Critical Inquiry*, 7, Nos. 1 and 4.

Mylne, Vivienne. *The Eighteenth-Century French Novel: Techniques of Illusion*. Manchester, Eng.: Manchester University Press, 1965.

Norris, Christopher. *Deconstruction: Theory and Practice*. London: Methuen, 1982.

Ouellet, Réal. "La Théorie du roman épistolaire en France au XVIIIe siècle." *Studies on Voltaire and the Eighteenth Century*, 89 (1962), 1209-27.

Piwowarczyk, Mary Ann. "The Narratee and the Situation of Enunciation: A Reconsideration of Prince's Theory." *Genre*, 9 (1976), 161-77.

———. "The Narratee in Selected Fictional Works of Diderot." Diss. University of Wisconsin 1978.

Pizzorusso, Arnaldo. "La Struttura delle *Liaisons dangereuses.*" In *Studi sulla letteratura dell'età preromantica in Francia*. Pisa: Goliardica, 1956.

Pomeau, René. *Laclos. Connaissance des Lettres*. Paris: Hatier, 1975.

Poulet, Georges. *The Interior Distance*. Baltimore: Johns Hopkins University Press, 1959.

Preston, John. *The Created Self: The Reader's Role in Eighteenth-Century Fiction*. London: Heinemann, 1970.

Prince, Gerald. "Introduction à l'étude du narrataire." *Poétique*, 14 (Oct. 1973), 177-96.

———. *Narratology: The Form and Functioning of Narrative*. Amsterdam: Mouton, 1982.

Rosbottom, Ronald. *Choderlos de Laclos*. TWAS, No. 502. Boston: Twayne Publishers, 1978.

Rosbottom, Ronald. "Dangerous Connections: A Communication Approach to the *Liaisons dangereuses.*" In *Laclos: Critical Approaches.* Ed. Lloyd Free. Pp. 183-221.

―――. "A Matter of Competence: The Relationship between Reading and Novel-Making in Eighteenth-Century France." *Studies in Eighteenth-Century Culture,* 6 (1977), 245-63.

―――. "Motifs in Epistolary Fiction: Analysis of a Sub-Genre." *L'Esprit Créateur,* 17 (1978), 279-301.

Rousset, Jean. *Forme et signification.* Paris: José Corti, 1962.

―――. "Les Lecteurs indiscrets." In *Laclos et le libertinage.* Ed. René Pomeau and Laurent Versini. Paris: Presses Universitaires de France, 1983, pp. 89-96.

―――. *Narcisse romancier: Essai sur la première personne dans le roman.* Paris: José Corti, 1973.

Rustin, Jacques. *Le Vice à la mode.* Association des Publications près les Universités de Strasbourg. Paris: Editions Ophrys, 1979.

Scholes, Robert. *Semiotics and Interpretation.* New Haven: Yale University Press, 1982.

Seylaz, Jean-Luc. *"Les Liaisons dangereuses" et la création romanesque chez Laclos.* Genève: Droz, 1958.

Showalter, English. *The Evolution of the French Novel.* Princeton: Princeton University Press, 1972.

Simon, John K. *Modern French Criticism: From Proust and Valéry to Structuralism.* Chicago: University of Chicago Press, 1972.

Stewart, Philip. *Imitation and Illusion in the French Memoir Novel, 1700-1750.* New Haven: Yale University Press, 1969.

―――. *Le Masque et la parole: Le Langage de l'amour au XVIIIe siècle.* Paris: José Corti, 1973.

Suleiman, Susan, and Inge Crossman, eds. *The Reader in the Text: Essays on Audience and Interpretation.* Princeton: Princeton University Press, 1980.

Thelander, Dorothy. *Laclos and the Epistolary Novel.* Genève: Droz, 1963.

Todorov, Tzvetan. "Les Catégories du récit littéraire." *Communications,* 8 (1966), 125-51.

―――. "Choderlos de Laclos et la théorie du récit." *Tel Quel,* 27 (1966), 17-28.

―――. *Introduction à la littérature fantastique.* Collection Points. Paris: Editions du Seuil, 1970.

―――. *Littérature et signification.* Langue et Langage. Paris: Larousse, 1967.

Selected Bibliography

Todorov, Tzvetan. *Poétique.* Collection Points. Paris: Editions du Seuil, 1973.

Tompkins, Jane, ed. *Reader-Response Criticism: From Formalism to Post-Structuralism.* Baltimore: Johns Hopkins University Press, 1980.

Turnell, Martin. *The Novel in France.* New York: New Directions, 1951.

Vailland, Roger. *Laclos par lui-même.* Ecrivains de Toujours. Paris: Editions du Seuil, 1953.

Van Rossum-Guyon, Françoise. "Point de vue ou perspective narrative: Théories et concepts critiques." *Poétique,* 4 (1970), 476-97.

Vartanian, Aram. "The Marquise de Merteuil: A Case of Mistaken Identity." *L'Esprit Créateur,* 3 (1963), 172-80.

Vernière, P. "*Les Liaisons dangereuses*: D'une morale des faits à une morale de la signification." In *Studies in 18th-Century French Literature Presented to Robert Niklaus.* Ed. Fox, Waddicor, and Watts. Exeter, Eng.: University of Exeter Press, 1975, pp. 295-305.

Versini, Laurent. *Laclos et la tradition: Essai sur les sources et la technique des "Liaisons dangereuses."* Paris: Klincksieck, 1968.

———. *Le Roman épistolaire.* Paris: Presses Universitaires de France, 1979.

Watt, Ian. *The Rise of the Novel: Studies in Defoe, Richardson, and Fielding.* 1957; rpt. Berkeley: University of California Press, 1967.

Wilson, W. Daniel. "Readers in Texts." *PMLA,* 96, No. 5 (Oct. 1981), 848-63.

Witkin, Sylvie Charron. "Laclos and Stendhal: Epistolary Communication and Communication between Author and Reader." Diss. University of Wisconsin 1982.

Wohlfarth, Irving. "The Irony of Criticism and the Criticism of Irony: A Study of Laclos Criticism." *Studies in Voltaire and the Eighteenth Century,* 120 (1974), 269-317.

In the PURDUE UNIVERSITY MONOGRAPHS IN ROMANCE LANGUAGES series the following monographs have been published thus far:

1. John R. Beverley: *Aspects of Góngora's "Soledades."*
   Amsterdam, 1980. xiv, 139 pp. Bound.

2. Robert Francis Cook: *"Chanson d'Antioche," chanson de geste: Le Cycle de la Croisade est-il épique?*
   Amsterdam, 1980. viii, 107 pp. Bound.

3. Sandy Petrey: *History in the Text: "Quatrevingt-Treize" and the French Revolution.*
   Amsterdam, 1980. viii, 129 pp. Bound.

4. Walter Kasell: *Marcel Proust and the Strategy of Reading.*
   Amsterdam, 1980. x, 125 pp. Bound.

5. Inés Azar: *Discurso retórico y mundo pastoral en la "Egloga segunda" de Garcilaso.*
   Amsterdam, 1981. x, 171 pp. Bound.

6. Roy Armes: *The Films of Alain Robbe-Grillet.*
   Amsterdam, 1981. x, 216 pp. Bound.

7. *Le "Galien" de Cheltenham,* edited by David M. Dougherty and Eugene B. Barnes.
   Amsterdam, 1981. xxxvi, 203 pp. Bound.

8. Ana Hernández del Castillo: *Keats, Poe, and the Shaping of Cortázar's Mythopoesis.*
   Amsterdam, 1981. xii, 135 pp. Bound.

9. Carlos Albarracín-Sarmiento: *Estructura del "Martín Fierro."*
   Amsterdam, 1981. xx, 336 pp. Bound.

10. C. George Peale et al. (eds.): *Antigüedad y actualidad de Luis Vélez de Guevara: Estudios críticos.*
    Amsterdam, 1983. xii, 298 pp. Bound.

11. David Jonathan Hildner: *Reason and the Passions in the "Comedias" of Calderón.*
    Amsterdam, 1982. xii, 119 pp. Bound.

PURDUE UNIVERSITY MONOGRAPHS IN ROMANCE LANGUAGES (Cont.)

12. Floyd Merrell: *Pararealities: The Nature of Our Fictions and How We Know Them.*
    Amsterdam, 1983. xii, 170 pp. Bound.

13. Richard E. Goodkin: *The Symbolist Home and the Tragic Home: Mallarmé and Oedipus.*
    Amsterdam, 1984. xvi, 203 pp. Paperbound.

14. Philip Walker: *"Germinal" and Zola's Philosophical and Religious Thought.*
    Amsterdam, 1984. xii, 157 pp. Paperbound.

15. Claire-Lise Tondeur: *Gustave Flaubert, critique: Thèmes et structures.*
    Amsterdam, 1984. xiv, 119 pp. Paperbound.

16. Carlos Feal: *En nombre de don Juan (Estructura de un mito literario).*
    Amsterdam, 1984. x, 175 pp. Paperbound.

17. Robert Archer: *The Pervasive Image: The Role of Analogy in the Poetry of Ausiàs March.*
    Amsterdam, 1985. xii, 220 pp. Paperbound.

18. Diana Sorensen Goodrich: *The Reader and the Text: Interpretative Strategies for Latin American Literatures.*
    Amsterdam, 1986. xii, 150 pp. Paperbound.

19. Lida Aronne-Amestoy: *Utopía, paraíso e historia: inscripciones del mito en García Márquez, Rulfo y Cortázar.*
    Amsterdam, 1986. xii, 167 pp. Paperbound.

20. Louise Mirrer-Singer: *The Language of Evaluation: A Sociolinguistic Approach to the Story of Pedro el Cruel in Ballad and Chronicle.*
    Amsterdam, 1986. xii, 128 pp. Paperbound.

21. Jo Ann Marie Recker: *"Appelle-moi 'Pierrot'": Wit and Irony in the "Lettres" of Madame de Sévigné.*
    Amsterdam, 1986. x, 128 pp. Paperbound.

22. J. H. Matthews: *André Breton: Sketch for an Early Portrait.*
    Amsterdam, 1986. xii, 176 pp. Paperbound.